427
TRU

DIALECTS

Second Edition

'The second edition of *Dialects* remains a useful and highly practical introduction to the study of dialects in the broadest sense of the term ... a clear and entertaining introduction which would be an excellent set text for A level and undergraduate work, and could supplement reading at more advanced stages.'

Joan Beal, University of Sheffield, UK

Routledge Language Workbooks provide absolute beginners with practical introductions to core areas of language study. Books in the series offer comprehensive coverage of the area as well as a basis for further investigation. Each Language Workbook guides the reader through the subject using 'hands-on' language analysis, equipping them with the basic analytical skills needed to handle a wide range of data. Written in a clear and simple style, with all technical concepts fully explained, Language Workbooks can be used for independent study or as part of a taught class.

Dialects

- introduces the many dialects of English spoken in the United Kingdom
- reveals the key issues engaged with in dialectology
- involves readers in collecting data
- contains numerous illustrative maps
- is written in a lively and engaging style, with information on 'posh' and 'less posh' dialects and spotting your dialect area

This newly revised edition of *Dialects* now features the International Phonetic Alphabet, used alongside simple representations of sounds, to explain pronunciations.

Peter Trudgill is Chair of English Linguistics at the University of Fribourg, Switzerland. His previous publications include: *Sociolinguistics: an introduction* (2000), *Alternative Histories of English* (co-edited with R. Watts, Routledge, 2001) and *English Accents and Dialects: an introduction to social and regional varieties of British English* (with A. Hughes, 1996).

LANGUAGE WORKBOOKS

Series editor: Richard Hudson

Books in the series:

Forthcoming:

DIALECTS

Second Edition

PETER TRUDGILL

Routledge
Taylor & Francis Group

LONDON AND NEW YORK

First published 1994
by Routledge
Reprinted 1996, 1999, 2002, 2003

Second edition first published 2004
by Routledge
2 Park Square, Milton Park, Abingdon, Oxon OX14 4RN

Simultaneously published in the USA and Canada by Routledge
270 Madison Avenue, New York, NY 10016

Routledge is an imprint of the Taylor & Francis Group

© 1994, 2004 Peter Trudgill

Typeset in Galliard and Futura by
Florence Production Ltd, Stoodleigh, Devon
Printed and bound in Great Britain by
TJ International Ltd, Padstow, Cornwall

All rights reserved. No part of this book may be reprinted or
reproduced or utilised in any form or by any electronic,
mechanical, or other means, now known or hereafter invented,
including photocopying and recording, or in any information
storage or retrieval system, without permission in writing from
the publishers.

British Library Cataloguing in Publication Data
A catalogue record for this book is available from
the British Library

Library of Congress Cataloging in Publication Data
A catalog record for this book has been requested

ISBN 0–415–34262–7 (hbk)
ISBN 0–415–34263–5 (pbk)

CONTENTS

USING THIS BOOK

This book covers a number of key issues in the field of dialectology, and involves readers actively in exploring them – in collecting data, in discovering patterns, and in thinking about general principles. It is intended for beginners who know only as much about dialects as any citizen does (i.e. a great deal), and it keeps the linguistic analysis of the data at the lowest possible level of technicality. If it is successful, readers should acquire a taste for *doing* dialectology; they should 'learn by doing', and be able to carry out themselves, in a modest and elementary way, the sorts of activities that academic linguists and dialectologists perform in their professional work.

The book is designed in the first instance for use in classes, and some of the suggested activities will involve the whole class. However, much of the work can also be done individually, so the book could also be used by an individual working alone. It is also aimed primarily at users in the United Kingdom, since all the examples are taken from British dialects of English.

Each chapter consists of a short discussion of general principles applied to some data, followed by a number of exercises. To get the full benefit of the book it is essential to try at least some of the exercises. The exercises are of two types: those for which data are provided, and those which require readers to find their own data. The first type provide the skills you need to analyse data, and model answers are provided at the back of the book. The second type take more time, but will be correspondingly more interesting, because readers will learn to apply the general principles to their own experience.

Readers whose appetites are sufficiently whetted to take the study of dialects further will find helpful pointers for further reading at the end of the book. Dialectology is a fascinating subject to read about, but it is one of the intentions of this book to show that it can be even more enjoyable to *do*.

A NOTE ON PHONETIC SYMBOLS

In order to derive the most benefit from this book, it will be useful, though by no means essential, to have some familiarity with the principles and practice of phonetic transcription. Phonetic transcriptions are used at a number of places in the book in order to indicate more precisely how words are pronounced than can be indicated by normal spelling. However, I have also always supplemented these transcriptions with renderings of pronunciations given in normal English orthography. These may be less clear or more ambiguous than the phonetic transcriptions, especially for the reader who is not already aware of how a particular English dialect sounds, but they are of course easier to read for people who have no familiarity with phonetic symbols.

Phonetic symbols are written between square brackets. The main principle of phonetic transcription is that only one letter is used for any one speech sound – and a single speech sound is always represented by the same letter and by no other. Thus, the consonant at the beginning of the word *cell* is transcribed phonetically with the symbol [s], while the consonant at the beginning of the word *comet* is transcribed with the symbol [k]. In English spelling, the letter *c* is sometimes pronounced 'hard' and sometimes 'soft', but in phonetic transcription there is no such ambiguity. In phonetic transcription there is no place for double letters representing a single sound – so that *Phil* is transcribed [fɪl], and *hiss* is transcribed [hɪs], while *his* is transcribed as [hɪz]. And we cannot use one letter to represent two sounds, so that *fix* is transcribed [fɪks]. There are of course also no 'silent letters' – *debt* is transcribed [dɛt].

Many of the phonetic symbols used in this book are identical in both form and sound to English letters. Symbols such as [d] and [m] should require no explanation. However, the following phonetic symbols do require some explanation, either because they are used in a particular way or because they are unfamiliar.

CONSONANTS

ŋ	as in	sing	sɪŋ
θ	as in	thick	θɪk
ð	as in	this	ðɪs
ʒ	as in	leisure	lɛʒə
g	not as in *gem* but as in	get	gɛt
x	the sound represented by *ch* in Scottish *loch* or German *acht*		
ɾ	a flapped r-sound as in Scottish *very* or Italian *vero*		
ʔ	a glottal stop, as in Cockney *better* 'be'er' bɛʔə		

VOWELS

ɪ	as in	kit	kɪt
ʊ	as in	foot	fʊt
ɛ	as in	dress	drɛs
æ	as in	trap	træp
ʌ	as in south of England	strut	strʌt
ɒ	as in	lot	lɒt
ə	as in	comma	kɒmə

Vowels which are long in their pronunciation are shown with a following [ː]

iː	as in	fleece	fliːs
ɔː	as in	law	lɔː
aː	as in	father	faːðə
eː	as in Scottish	bay	beː

Diphthongs are vowels which change their quality during their pronunciaton. They are transcribed by indicating the sound with which they begin and the sound with which they end, so that [æɪ] indicates a diphthong which begins with the vowel of *trap* and ends with the vowel of *kit*.

aʊ	as in	mouth	maʊθ
aɪ	as in	price	praɪs

This book uses only a very small subset of the symbols of the International Phonetic Alphabet, which is designed to make possible the phonetic description of the sounds of all the world's languages. For more on this, see *Speech Sounds* by Patricia Ashby (also in the Language Workbooks series).

STUDYING ENGLISH DIALECTS

> Like all languages, English is very varied. It comes in many different regional and social varieties. All these varieties are linguistically equivalent. No variety of the language is linguistically superior to any other.

Some English words
sidewalk, chiyack
rone, ashet, faucet
sophomore, dreich

We are very used to talking about our language as if it were a single, clearly defined entity: *the* English Language. Looked at in one way, this is only sensible, particularly when we think of the written language. English is a language which has its own literature, its own grammar books, and its own dictionaries. It is also a language which is quite clearly not French, not German, not Chinese – or any other language. To talk about the English language does actually mean something.

This view of English can be rather misleading, though. It is equally sensible, looked at in another way, to claim that there is no such thing as the English language, if by that we were to mean that there was only one way to speak or write English. The point is that English – like all other languages – comes in many different forms, particularly when we think of the spoken language – and in this book we are concentrating on spoken English. Anyone can tell that the English of the British Isles is different from the English of the United States or Australia. The English of England is clearly different from the English of Scotland or Wales. The English of Lancashire is noticeably different from the English of Northumberland or Kent. And the English of Liverpool is not the same as the English of Manchester. There is very considerable regional variation within the English language as it is spoken in different parts of the British Isles and different parts of the world. The fact is that the way you speak English has a lot to do with *where you are from* – where you grew up and first learnt your language. If you grew up in Liverpool, your English will be different from the English of Manchester, which will in turn be different from the English of London, and so on.

Where you are from, of course, will not be the only thing which influences how you speak. People speak different kinds of English depending on what kind of social background they come from, so that some Liverpool speakers may be 'more Liverpudlian' than others, and some Manchester people may be easier to identify as Mancunians than others. Some speakers may even be so 'posh' that it is not possible to tell where they come from at all (we shall discuss this further in **Unit 2**).

Dialect   These social and geographical kinds of language are known as DIALECTS. Dialects, then, have to do with a speaker's social and geographical origins – and we are talking here about *all* speakers. It is important to emphasise that everybody speaks a dialect. Dialects are not peculiar or old-fashioned or rustic ways of speaking. They are not something which only other people have. Just as everybody comes from somewhere and has a particular kind of social background, so everybody – including you – speaks a dialect. Your dialect is the particular combination of English words, pronunciations and grammatical forms that you share with other people from your area and your social background, and that differs in certain ways from the combination used by people from other areas and backgrounds.

It is also important to point out that none of these combinations – none of these dialects – is linguistically superior in any way to any other. We may as individuals be rather fond of our own dialect. This should not make us think, though, that it is actually any better than any other dialect. Dialects are not good or bad, nice or nasty, right or wrong – they are just different from one another, and it is the mark of a civilised society that it tolerates different dialects just as it tolerates different races, religions and sexes. American English is not better – or worse – than British English. The dialect of BBC newsreaders is not linguistically superior to the dialect of Bristol dockers or Suffolk farmworkers. There is nothing you can do or say in one dialect that you cannot do or say in another dialect.

Dialectologist   Scientists who study dialects – DIALECTOLOGISTS – start from the assumption that all dialects are linguistically equal. (We will discuss the issue of social equality in **Unit 3**.) What dialectologists are interested in are differences between dialects. The task of dialectologists is to describe different dialects, to note differences between them, and, importantly, to try and explain how these differences came about. We shall be looking at different aspects of the dialectologist's work in subsequent units.

Most people who have grown up somewhere in the English-speaking world are already rather good English dialectologists, even if they have never studied English dialectology. During our lives, we become familiar with a wider and wider range of varieties of English and are usually able to tell quite a lot about a person we meet for the first time simply from the way they speak. Their words, grammar and pronunciation tell us things about their regional and social background. In the following exercises, you are asked to say what you can about the origins of the texts in question.

EXERCISES

1.1 What is the regional origin of the following poem?

> The wuid-reek mells wi the winter haar
> And aa the birds are gane;
> They're burnan the leaves, the treen are bare,
> December rules a dour domain.
>
> The wuid-reek draws a memorie
> Frae some far neuk in the brain
> When I was a loun and hadna loed
> And never kent the world's bane.
>
> Och, burn the leaves and burn the branch
> And burn the holly treen!
> O winter, burn the hairt I want –
> And syne burn mine again!

1.2 What is the regional origin of the following passage? Make a list of the words and spellings which led you to make this identification.

> She must have felt me staring at her, for she turned around, and her eyes, which were an astonishing color, now looked at me with an open small-town concern. And now I realized the detective had seen me chatting with nothing less than a blonde. We stepped into a squad car, the siren was turned on, and we drove to an exit, and then turned back to the apartment. By the time we arrived, there were two more squad cars in the street. Our silence continued as we rode up in the elevator, and when we got to the apartment, a few more detectives and a few more police were standing around. There was a joyless odor in the air.

1.3 What is the regional origin of the following passage? Make a list of the features which led you to make this identification.

> I've lost my pal, 'e's the best in all the tahn,
> But don't you fink 'im dead, becos 'e ain't.
> But since he's wed, 'e 'as ter nuckle dahn,
> It's enough ter vex the temper of a saint.
> E's a brewer's drayman, wiv a leg of mutton fist,
> An' as strong as a bullick or an horse.
> Yet in 'er 'ands 'e's like a little kid,
> Oh! I wish as I could get him a divorce.

1.4 The following words mean different things in American and British English. Find out what the differences are:

nervy, scrappy, pavement, homely, momentarily, cheap

1.5 The following English words have at least two different pronunciations in different varieties of the language. Say what they are:

dance, butter, bath, off, card, head, plant, one, supper, girl

1.6 Watch an American TV programme, for example, a comedy or crime show, and an Australian TV programme, for example, a soap opera, and make a note of all the words and expressions which strike you as being distinctively American and Australian. Discuss these words and expressions.

POSH AND LESS POSH DIALECTS

2

> Dialects are both regional and social. The dialect with the greatest prestige is Standard English, which has slightly different forms in different parts of the English-speaking world. It can be spoken with any kind of accent or pronunciation.

Some English sentences
She don't want none of that.
We ain't got none of them sweets.
He's the one what done it.

In the first unit, we saw that what sort of dialect you speak depends on your social and regional background. In this unit we look at the relationship between SOCIAL AND REGIONAL DIALECTS, which in Britain is a rather complicated one.

Social and regional dialects

There is no doubt that the dialect of English which has the highest social status is the dialect which is widely known as STANDARD ENGLISH. Standard English is the dialect which is normally used in printed books and newspapers; it is the dialect used in the education system; and it is the dialect found in dictionaries and grammar books. Standard English uses grammatical forms such as:

Standard English

I don't want any.
She hasn't done it.
those people over there
They did it yesterday.
the person who went
He hurt himself.

Nonstandard dialects

NONSTANDARD DIALECTS, on the other hand, are dialects which use grammatical forms such as:

I don't want none.
She ain't done it.
them people over there
They done it yesterday.
the person what went
He hurt hisself.

Forms such as these are not 'wrong' in any way and should not be regarded as 'mistakes'. They are used by millions of English speakers around the world, and are representative of grammatical systems that are different from Standard English, not linguistically inferior to it. (We will discuss the grammar of nonstandard dialects further in **Units 9, 10** and **11**.)

The normal social convention what we operates with in the English-speaking world be that writing, particularly writing intended for publication, should be done in Standard English. This here book ain't no exception – it be writ in Standard English. This, however, be a matter of social convention. There ain't nothing what you can say nor write in Standard English what can't be said nor writ in other dialects. That's why we's writ this here paragraph in a nonstandard dialect, just to make the point.

On the other hand, there is no doubt that nonstandard dialect forms have less prestige than Standard English constructions. This is hardly surprising, since the Standard English dialect is spoken natively by British people who can be regarded as being at the 'top' of the social scale, in the sense that they have more money, influence, education and prestige than people lower down the social scale.

The Standard English dialect itself is not entirely uniform. Scottish Standard English, for example, is clearly different from the Standard English of England at a number of points. It uses words such as *outwith* 'outside', *rone* 'drainpipe', and *ashet* 'serving dish' which are not known in England or Wales. And Scottish Standard English speakers also use grammatical forms that are not found in the Standard English elsewhere, such as:

Had you a good time last night?
My clothes need washed.

and

Will I shut the door?

whereas similar speakers in England and Wales would say:

Did you have a good time last night?
My clothes need washing.

and

Shall I shut the door?

There are also differences between the north and south of England. In the south, for example, people are more likely to say:

I haven't seen him.
She won't do it.

while in the north of England you are more likely to hear people say:

I've not seen him.
She'll not do it.

Generally speaking, however, there is relatively little geographical variation within Standard English. It is as you go further down the social scale that regional differences become more apparent. The most regional of regional dialect forms are to be found at the 'bottom' of the social scale. Thus, the Standard English relative pronoun *who* corresponds to a number of different nonstandard forms in different parts of the country:

Standard English dialect
the woman who taught us

Nonstandard dialects
the woman what taught us
the woman as taught us
the woman at taught us
the woman which taught us

This relationship between social and regional variation, with more regional variation at the bottom of the social scale and less at the top, also applies to ACCENTS. In this book we make a distinction between **Accent** dialect and accent. Accent simply refers to pronunciation. Your accent is the way you pronounce English when you speak it – and of course everybody therefore has an accent. Your dialect, on the other hand, has to do also with the grammatical forms that you use, as well, perhaps, as any regional vocabulary that you employ.

It is important to make this distinction between dialect and accent, in order to be able to show that it is possible to speak Standard English with a regional accent. Standard English has nothing to do with pronunciation. In fact, most people who speak Standard English do so with some form of regional pronunciation, so that you can tell where they come from much more by their accent than by their grammar or vocabulary. There is only a small minority of the population, perhaps 3 to 5 per cent, who speak Standard English with the totally regionless accent we sometimes call the 'BBC' accent. Here again, the further down the social scale you go, the more regional differences in accent you will find. The upper classes who speak with a 'BBC' accent do not betray their geographical origins at all when they speak, although of course they do give lots of clues about their social origins! People of a more middle-class background will tend to have more of a regional accent, but you might not be able to say any more about them than that they sound to you as if they come from, say, Yorkshire or East Anglia. And with people from nearer the bottom of the social scale you might be able to say, if they have 'broader' or even more regional accents, that they come from, say, Huddersfield or Ipswich.

EXERCISES

2.1 Convert the nonstandard dialect passage on page 6 above into the Standard English dialect.

2.2 State which of the following sentences are in Standard English and which are in some nonstandard dialect.

(a) We don't want to do that.

(b) He don't want to do that.

(c) They always behave very nice to me.

(d) They always seem very nice to me.

(e) I'm very sorry – I'm afraid we haven't got none left.

(f) I'm very sorry – I'm afraid we've got none left.

(g) I know what I have to do.

(h) I know there's work what I have to do.

(i) We done that quite recently.

(j) We've done that quite recently.

(k) 'E doesn't like 'is new 'ouse.

(l) He don't like his new house.

2.3 In different parts of Britain, people have different preferences as to how they contract verb phrases containing *not*. For example, *I have not done it* can be either *I've not done it* or *I haven't done it*. Discuss which of the following alternatives you prefer:

He won't do it.	He'll not do it.
She isn't coming.	She's not coming.
You're not coming?	You aren't coming?
We haven't seen it.	We've not seen it.
She hasn't read it.	She's not read it.

If there are people in your group from different areas, try and work out what the regional distribution of the different forms is.

2.4 In different parts of Britain, a number of different sentence structures are used. Which of the following alternatives do you use?

I want out.	I want to go out.
I want my hair cutting.	I want my hair cut.
I've finished it.	I'm finished it.
My hair needs cutting.	My hair needs cut.
I'm just coming.	I'm now coming.
I was sat outside.	I was sitting outside.

If there are people in your group from different areas, try and work out what the regional distribution of the different forms is.

2.5 Convert the following nonstandard sentences into Standard English:

(a) I don't want none of that.

(b) Them tapes aren't no good.

(c) He give it to me last night.

(d) It weren't John I seen.

(e) They done what they was supposed to.

(f) That's the one what I want.

(g) We always goes there on Saturdays.

(h)   You writ that very quick!

(i)   It were him as told me.

(j)   I know I shouldn't have went.

2.6   As we saw above, Standard English comes in a number of different forms. Consider the following Standard English constructions, and say what part of the English-speaking world they are most likely to come from:

(a)   I'll give it him.

(b)   Have you ever gone to London?

(c)   Going away tomorrow he is.

(d)   He ordered the town evacuated.

(e)   The dog wants out.

(f)   I'll come see you soon.

(g)   We'd a good time last week.

(h)   It was very ill that he looked.

2.7   Discuss why it is, given that Standard English is so widely used in education and in the media, that most people in Britain continue to speak nonstandard dialects.

ENGLISH IN MANY SHAPES AND FORMS

3

In addition to regional and social dialects and accents, English also has different styles, which are used in different social situations, and different registers, which are used for different topics.

A piece of English prose

Proguanil is effective against the tissue forms of some strains of *P.falciparum* and acts through an active metabolic cycloguanil. The mechanism of action is probably due to inhibition of dihydrofolate reductase. The effect of this action is to prevent schizogony and its main effect is against the developing primary tissue schizonts.

Dialects involve differences within the English language which have to do with where speakers grow up, and what sort of social background they come from. But there are also other sorts of difference within the English language, and in this unit we look at these differences and show that it is important to be able to distinguish between them and dialect differences.

For example, regardless of what dialect people speak, they will use different sorts of language depending on what sort of social situation they find themselves in. No one uses exactly the same kind of English when they are talking to their friends in a café or pub as when they are talking to strangers in a more formal situation.

STYLES

Situational varieties of English of this type are known as *styles*, and stylistic variation can be thought of as taking place along a kind of sliding scale of formality. Styles of English range from very formal to very informal, with a whole continuum of varieties in between. Most often, differences between styles have to do with words, with very informal or colloquial **Slang** vocabulary often being referred to as SLANG. For example, *fatigued* is a very formal word, while *tired* is an intermediate or neutral word, while *knackered* is a very informal or slang word. They all mean the same thing, but they are stylistically very different.

> My companion is exceedingly fatigued.

has the same meaning as

> My friend is extremely tired.

which has the same meaning as

> My mate is bloody knackered.

But these three different sentences would be used in very different social situations, and produce different sorts of social effects.

It is important to notice, also, that *style* and *dialect* are independent of one another. It is true, of course, that the Standard English dialect is more likely to be used on formal public occasions where formal styles are also more likely to be used. But there is no necessary connection between Standard English and formal styles, or nonstandard dialects and informal styles.

> My mate is bloody knackered.

is informal style, as we saw above, but it is also Standard English. On the other hand,

> My friend be very tired.

which is stylistically less informal, is not in Standard English but some other dialect.

REGISTERS

There is another kind of variation within English, which is independent of both dialect and style. This has to do with the topic that the speaker is talking about. Kinds of language that reflect the subject being talked **Register** or written about are known as REGISTERS. These, too, have most often got to do with vocabulary. The language or register of medicine, for example, contains words such as:

> appendectomy, clavicle *and* rubella.

The register of law includes words such as:

> tort, hereinafter *and* felony.

The register of football consists of words such as:

> midfield, one-two *and* corner.

And the register of car mechanics has words such as:

> torque, tappets *and* clutch.

The more TECHNICAL REGISTERS, such as that of medicine, raise an interesting point. Obviously, if you are going to be able to talk about a particular topic successfully, you need to learn the vocabulary that goes with that topic. If you don't know the special meaning that the word *corner* has in soccer, there are obviously still things you have to learn about the game. Part of learning physical geography is knowing what an *esker* is. And studying geometry will inevitably involve you in learning what *hypotenuse* means. But it is also true that you can discuss *having your appendix out*, or your *collarbone*, or *German measles* without acquiring the technical register of medicine. Part of the reason for saying *clavicle* rather than *collarbone* is to show that you are an insider in the medical profession. In other words, registers may have a social as well as linguistic function – they show who is a member of the in-group and who is not. Outsiders often react to this by calling insiders' registers JARGON. If you think that *appendectomy* is 'jargon', you are probably not a doctor.

Technical register

Jargon

It is not necessary to use Standard English in order to speak formally. Neither is there any necessary connection between Standard English and technical registers. It is quite possible for Standard English speakers to swear and use slang vocabulary, just as it is possible for nonstandard speakers to use a whole range of styles. The independence of style, register and dialect can be seen in the following example:

> *Standard English dialect*

He hasn't broken his clavicle.	*neutral style, technical register*
He hasn't broken his collarbone.	*neutral style, nontechnical*
He hasn't bust his clavicle.	*informal style, technical*
He hasn't bust his collarbone.	*informal style, nontechnical*

Nonstandard dialect

He ain't broke his clavicle.	*neutral style, technical register*
He ain't broke his collarbone.	*neutral style, nontechnical*
He ain't bust his clavicle.	*informal style, technical*
He ain't bust his collarbone.	*informal style, nontechnical*

EXERCISES

3.1 Convert the following passage into a more informal style:

> Mother was somewhat displeased when she observed that I had omitted to remove my soiled garments from the kitchen and place them in a more appropriate location, a task which I had given her an undertaking that I would perform before Father's return from his place of employment.

3.2 Suppose that the following passage of prose was produced by a school pupil in response to a request to write a paragraph in Standard English and in a formal style. Identify features of (a) nonstandard dialect; (b) informal style; and (c) lack of knowledge of the appropriate register.

> When my old man come home last night, he was really bushed. He sat and watched telly all evening. I done my homework and then watched television too. An operator doctor was talking about the Health Service. It was really boring. Then there was the one in charge of hospitals. He wasn't very interesting neither.

3.3 Label the following sentences according to their dialect (standard or nonstandard), register (technical or nontechnical) and style (formal or informal).

(a) I wants you to play this melody allegro, not adagio.

(b) I want you to play this tune quickly, not slowly.

(c) The rear off-side wheel looks a bit wobbly.

(d) The back left-hand wheel seems to be oscillating somewhat.

(e) His patella sustained an injury.

(f) He done his knee cap in.

(g) The publican don't need no more firkins.

(h) The landlord doesn't need any more small barrels.

(i)   She ain't attended no baptisms.

(j)   She hasn't been to any christenings.

3.4 Convert the following passage of prose into a less technical register and a more neutral style, using a dictionary if necessary:

> If the regular premium tendered on a due date is greater than the existing aggregate regular premium on that due date, the company will issue a supplementary schedule on which the increment regular premium will be the amount by which the regular premium tendered exceeds the existing aggregate regular premium; provided that, if waiver of premium benefit is specified in the plan schedule as available, or there is an increase in the life cover, the issue of the supplementary schedule will be subject to evidence satisfactory to the company as to the continued insurability of the life assured for waiver of premium benefit or life cover on the existing terms.

3.5 It is of course not just professions such as law or medicine that have technical, specialised registers. Consider some informal or nonacademic activity, sport or hobby that you know something about, such as car mechanics, knitting, train-spotting, football, music or cooking, and make a list of technical terms associated with this activity that people who know nothing about the subject might not know or understand.

3.6 Invent examples of stylistically inappropriate greetings to different kinds of people such as friends, teachers, parents, shop assistants, etc.

3.7 Identify the style and register of the following passage, and list the features which led you to make this identification:

> The ground was bare ice polished by the wind, with scattered pebbles embedded in it. As it steepened, the slope became covered with brick-hard snow on which I found that my short-pointed crampons tended to scrape and slip. I was heading for a snow-filled gully or couloir. The ridge now towered directly above our heads. The sherpa wanted me to move farther to the right, to the foot of the ridge before it reaches the edge of the col, and from the point we had reached the gully appeared to rise so steeply that for a moment I was inclined to agree that we might as well

try the alternative rock climb. But it would now have involved a long detour to the right, and there was a compelling urge to economise energy as much as possible. Indeed we already had little in reserve. We stopped to take our first rest, sitting in a shallow groove of an incipient bergschrund which marks a sudden steepening of the gully.

3.8 Identify the style and register of the following passage, and list the features which led you to make this identification:

It is the business of epistemology to arrange the propositions which constitute our knowledge in a certain logical order, in which the later propositions are accepted because of their logical relation to those that came before them. It is not necessary that the later propositions should be logically deducible from the earlier ones; what is necessary is that the earlier ones should supply whatever grounds exist for thinking it likely that the later ones are true. When we are considering empirical knowledge, the earliest propositions in the hierarchy are not deduced from the other propositions, and yet are not mere arbitrary assumptions. They have grounds, though their grounds are not propositions, but observed occurrences. Such propositions, as observed above, I shall call *basic* propositions; they fulfil the function assigned by the logical positivists to what they call *protocol propositions*.

DIALECTS – THE OLD AND THE NEW

4

Dialects of English can be divided into two types: Traditional Dialects, which are most often spoken by older people in geographically peripheral, more rural parts of the country, and Mainstream Dialects, which are more like Standard English, and are more associated with younger, urban speakers.

Some English words
lewze, mawther, eft
mistall, loup, laik
bairn, shippon, fainites
nesh, thole, keek

In this unit we make a distinction between TRADITIONAL DIALECTS and MAINSTREAM DIALECTS. Traditional Dialects are what most people generally think of when they hear the term 'dialect'. People tend to think of them as being 'real' or 'genuine' or 'pure' dialects. They also tend to imagine that they are spoken only in rural areas.

It is certainly true that Traditional Dialects are much more prevalent in rural areas than they are in urban ones, although there are some urban dialects, particularly in Scotland, that are Traditional in type. And they are easier to find in those parts of the country which are furthest away from London: the southwest of England, parts of northern England, the Lowlands of Scotland, and areas of Northern Ireland. (Traditional Dialects of English have never been spoken in the Highlands of Scotland or in most of Wales, because these areas were originally Gaelic and Welsh speaking, respectively, and became bilingual or monolingual English speaking only relatively recently.)

Traditional Dialects are mostly, but by no means exclusively, spoken by older people, and are clearly gradually disappearing – they are being

**Traditional
Dialect**

**Mainstream
Dialect**

replaced by Mainstream Dialects. Their most typical characteristic, however, is that they are linguistically very different from one another and from Standard English. Mainstream Dialects, on the other hand, which are spoken by a majority of the population, particularly younger speakers in urban areas, are linguistically more similar to one another and to Standard English. Standard English itself has to be considered a Mainstream Dialect.

For example,

> She's not going.
> She isn't going.

and

> She ain't going.

are all Mainstream Dialect forms, although the first two are Standard and the third Nonstandard. On the other hand,

> She byun't a-goin.
> Hoo inno goin.

and

> Her bain't a-goin.

are typical Traditional Dialect forms. Most people have never heard such forms used, although it is perfectly possible to find speakers of such dialects if you know where to look.

In pronunciation, too, we can see the same sorts of differences. In different parts of the country, accents associated with Mainstream Dialects might pronounce a word like *bone* as **bown** or **bawn** or **boun** [boʊn, bɔːn, baʊn]. On the other hand, Traditional Dialect pronunciations might include **bwoon** or **bane** or **bee-yan** [bwʊn, beːn, biən].

To make this point clearer, we can point out that it is at the level of Mainstream Dialects that you find accent differences of the following types:

1 In the Midlands and north of England, and some areas of northern Wales, *put* and *but* rhyme, and words like *cut, hush, mud,* on the one hand, and words like *foot, push, could,* on the other, have the same vowel. In the south of England, and in Scotland and Northern Ireland, *put* and *but* do not rhyme, and the two sets of words have different vowels.

2 In southwestern England, parts of Lancashire, Scotland and Ireland, the *r* in words like *car*, *for* and *butter* is actually pronounced. In the other areas of England it is not, so that these words sound like **cah** [kaː], **faw** [fɔː], and **butta** [bʌtə].

3 In most of England and Wales, people with local accents don't always pronounce *h* in words like *house*, *hill* and *hat*. In Ireland, Scotland, Northumberland, Durham and parts of East Anglia, the local accents still consistently preserve the pronunciation with *h*.

On the other hand, Traditional Dialect pronunciations which can no longer be found in the Mainstream Dialects include the following:

1 In the southwestern peninsula of England, words which begin in the spelling with *f*, *s*, *sh* are pronounced with **v**, **z**, **zh** [v, z, ʒ]. So *farmer* is pronounced **varmer**, *Somerset* is **Zummerzet** and *sheep* is **zheep** [ʒiːp].

2 In the Lowlands of Scotland, Northern Ireland, Northumberland, Cumbria, Durham and north Yorkshire, words like *long*, *wrong*, *song* are pronounced **lang**, **rang**, **sang**.

3 In the Lowlands of Scotland and Northern Ireland, words like *night*, *right*, *light* are pronounced **nicht** [nɪxt], **richt**, **licht** with the **ch** [x] sound that you find in German. In Northumberland, Cumbria, Durham, Yorkshire, and parts of Lincolnshire, Nottinghamshire and Derbyshire, they are pronounced **neet** [niːt], **reet**, **leet**.

The following exercises emphasise the point that Traditional Dialects can be very different from the Mainstream Dialects, including Standard English.

EXERCISES

4.1 Convert the following Traditional (East Anglian) Dialect passage into Standard English.

> I reckon yow wonder why I han't writ lately. Well, Aunt Agatha she ha been a-spring-cleanin', and we ha wery nigh finished. She ha got only one more place to do – that's outside (that's the coal shud). Granfa he mob. He say yow can't see no difference when that's done, only yow can't find nothin'. But he lend a hand. We all got fit, when Aunt Agatha found she'd lent her whitewawsh brush to Mrs. W.,

so I had to go ahter that. Well, bor, she say to me 'Thank yar Aunt Agatha for the use of the brush. I ha got a new one now so I shall neither want to borra nor yit lend'. She gan me some peppermint cooshies for Granfa. He mobbed. He say 'I don't want them things'.

4.2   Convert the following Traditional (Lowland Scots) Dialect passage into Standard English.

A man canna get his meat taen for thinkin' will it be aye, or will it be no. Afore lang he doesna richtly care which o' them it is if only it wad be ane o' the twa an' be dune wi' 't. And if there's a thing ye're feart o', and its comin', and no comin', and never comin' – man, dae ye ken efter a while ye wad be gled o' it comin', ye wad even gang halfroads to meet it, only for no tae hae it comin', and no comin'.

4.3   Convert the following Traditional (Wearside) Dialect verse into Standard English prose.

Mark Fortin' at steeith had just moored his keel,
And the neet was that dark it wad freeten the deil;
Ye could not see yer thumbe eff ye held up yer hand,
When Mark started off for ti come ower land.
He called at the Reed Dog, but he didn't stay lang,
Smoked his pipe, had some talk, an' sung a bit sang;
He'd had nowt ti drink for ti mak him feel queer –
On'y two pots o' rum and three quairts o' beer.

4.4   Convert the following Traditional Dialect poem, by the Dorset poet William Barnes, into Standard English prose.

The wold clock's feäce is still in pleäce,
Wi' hands a-stealen round,
His bob do swing an' bell do ring,
As when I heärd his sound,
A-leäven hwome, so long a-gone,
An' left en there, a-ticken on.

Noo doust do clog, noo rust uncog
His wheels to keep em still,
Noo blow ha' veil to crack his bell
That still do ringle shrill.
I wish that I'd a-gone so well
'S the clock's wold bob, an' wheels, an' bell.

Who now do wind his chaïn, a-twin'd
As he do run his hours,
Or meäke a gloss to sheen across
His door, wi' goolden flow'rs,
Since he've a-sounded out the last
Still hours our dear good mother pass'd?

4.5 Look at the twelve 'English words' at the beginning of this unit, and try and find out what they mean, by consulting dictionaries or other sources, if necessary.

4.6 Discuss pronunciations which are typical of the Traditional and Mainstream Dialects of your own part of the country.

5 DIALECT MAPS

Dialects can be studied by large-scale dialect surveys, such as the Survey of English Dialects, which use various methodological techniques for getting information from dialect speakers, and for producing maps of the distribution of dialect features.

Some questions from the Survey of English Dialects

What do you call the short stiff hairs on the back of a pig?

What do you call this?

What do you call the male of the cow?

Two bad-tempered dogs when they meet usually begin to . . .

Survey of English Dialects (SED)

Linguistic Survey of Scotland

A lot of what we know about the Traditional Dialects of the United Kingdom comes from work carried out by the SURVEY OF ENGLISH DIALECTS (SED), based at the University of Leeds, and the LINGUISTIC SURVEY OF SCOTLAND (which also investigated Northern Ireland), based at Edinburgh University. In this unit, we look at the sort of work which dialect surveys of this type carry out.

In order to find out about the Traditional Dialects of England, the Survey of English Dialects during the 1950s sent trained fieldworkers to more than 300 different places, nearly all of them country villages, in all parts of England. In each village, they found people, usually but not always older people, who spoke the local dialect and who were willing to help, and interviewed them, usually for many hours.

It was important, of course, to get the same information from each of the locations that the fieldworkers went to, so to make sure this happened all the workers had the same questionnaire that they used with their local informants. Here are just a few of the questions that were asked.

What do you call the man who looks after those animals that give us wool? [*shepherd*]

What do you put up in a field to frighten birds away? [*scarecrow*]

If I didn't know what a cowman is, you would tell me: He is the man . . . looks after the cows. [*that*]

What do you call a dog with half a dozen breeds in it? [*mongrel*]

What do you call this? [showing a picture of a *plough*]

You will see that many of the words that the survey was interested in had to do with farming and other aspects of rural life. One reason for this was that many such words were dying out, with more mechanised farming practices, and they wanted to record as many such words as possible. More importantly, perhaps, you will also see that they didn't ask questions like 'What do you call a shepherd?' or 'What do you call the man who looks after the sheep?' This was because they didn't want to put words or pronunciations into people's minds. What they were after was the local Traditional Dialect, uninfluenced by Standard English or other Mainstream Dialects.

This is part of a well-known problem to do with carrying out research into dialects. This problem is known to dialectologists as the OBSERVER'S PARADOX. This means that what dialectologists really want to do is to observe how people speak when they are not being observed. The point is, of course, that if people know that you are studying the way they speak, they may become self-conscious and start speaking in an unnatural manner. It is therefore important, if you are carrying out a study of dialects, especially if you are using a tape-recorder, to put people at their ease and make them feel comfortable about the way they speak, and your interest in them, their area, and their dialect.

Observers' Paradox

When all the SED information was in, the responses to each of the questions could be grouped together and published. This meant that anybody – including of course the workers on the Survey themselves – who wanted to draw maps for features that they were especially interested in, could now do so. Some of the maps that have been prepared are concerned with differences of vocabulary. Map 5.1, for example, is an SED map for the word used in different dialects for a thin piece of wood of the sort that you can get stuck in a finger. You might like to check and see if the one given for your area is a word you know or use yourself. The lines on the map which divide an area which has one word from an area which has another are called ISOGLOSSES by dialectologists.

Isogloss

Map 5.2, on the other hand, is a map which is concerned with a grammatical feature. This is a map prepared by the SED showing forms corresponding to Standard English *we are*. You can see that in addition

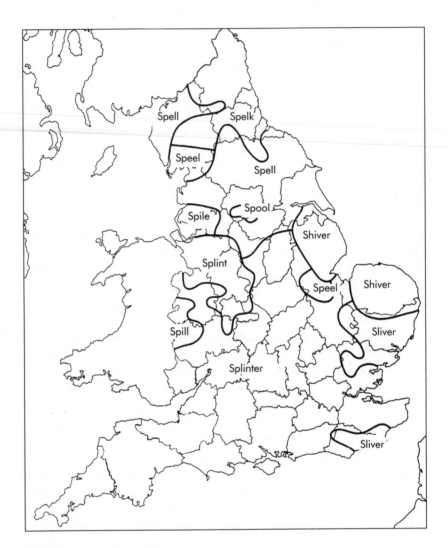

5.1
Words for
Splinter in English
Dialects

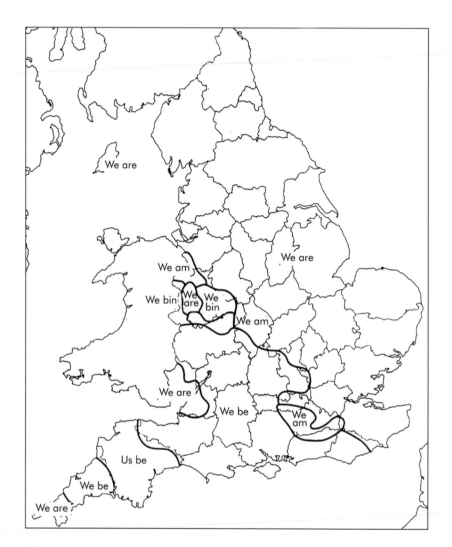

5.2
We are in
Traditional
Dialects

Last has the
vowel of bat
[æ]

Last has the
vowel of father
[ɑ:]

5.3
Different
pronunciation of
Last in the north
and south of
England

to *we are*, Traditional Dialects also have, in different parts of England, a number of other forms: *we am*, *we bin*, *we be*, and *us be*.

Map 5.3 gives information on pronunciation – on different accents. The map shows areas in the north of England where the word *last* has the same short **a** sound [æ] as in *bat*, while in areas to the south it has the same long **a** [aː] vowel as *father*. This is, of course, a difference which is found not only in Traditional Dialects but also in Mainstream Dialects. In England, northern and southern accents alike agree in having the short **a** in *bat*, *sad*, *cash*, and in having the long **a** in *father*, *banana*, *lager*. There is another group of words, however, which, like *last*, can easily be used to tell if a speaker comes from the north or south of England. There are a few hundred of these words, but they include *path*, *grass*, *laugh*, *dance*, *grant*, *sample*, *demand*.

EXERCISES

5.1   Here are some data from an informal dialect survey which examined the local word for gym-shoes or trainers in different parts of the country. Use these data to draw a map of Britain which marks isoglosses indicating the areas in which the different forms are used.

Aberdeen	sandshoes	Exeter	plimsolls
Aylesbury	pumps	Glasgow	sandshoes
Ayr	sandshoes	Gloucester	daps
Bedford	plimsolls	Grimsby	plimsolls
Belfast	gutties	Halifax	pumps
Birkenhead	gollies	Huddersfield	pumps
Birmingham	pumps	Hull	sandshoes
Blackburn	pumps	Ipswich	plimsolls
Bournemouth	plimsolls	Leeds	pumps
Bradford	pumps	Leicester	pumps
Brighton	plimsolls	London	plimsolls
Bristol	daps	Manchester	pumps
Cambridge	plimsolls	Newcastle	sandshoes
Cardiff	daps	Northampton	pumps
Carlisle	pumps	Northwich	pumps
Chester	gollies	Norwich	plimsolls
Dover	plimsolls	Nottingham	pumps
Dundee	sandshoes	Oxford	daps
Dungannon	gutties	Peterborough	plimsolls
Durham	sandshoes	Reading	plimsolls
Edinburgh	sandshoes	Salisbury	plimsolls

Scunthorpe	pumps	Swindon	daps
Sheffield	pumps	Tynemouth	sandshoes
Southampton	plimsolls	Ullapool	sandshoes
Southend	plimsolls	Ventnor	plimsolls
Stevenage	plimsolls	Walsall	pumps
Stirling	sandshoes	Whitehaven	pumps
Stoke	pumps	Woking	plimsolls
Sunderland	sandshoes	Wolverhampton	pumps
Swansea	daps		

5.2 List as many words as you can, in addition to those cited above on page 27, which are spelt with the letter *a* and which have a different pronunciation in the north and the south of England.

5.3 List twenty words which are spelt with the letter *u* which have a different pronunciation in the north and the south of England. (Speakers from the north of England may find this harder to do than speakers from elsewhere in the British Isles – consult a pronouncing dictionary if necessary.)

5.4 Plan a short questionnaire for the study of dialects in your own area.

5.5 Discuss and make a list of dialect words used in your own area.

WHAT DIALECT MAPS CAN TELL US

6

Maps showing the geographical distribution of dialect features can be interpreted to give us interesting information. Distributions, for example, can be explained in terms of settlement patterns and other historical events.

Some Norwegian words for food
egg, brød, melk, fisk
lamm, krabbe, eple, kake
lever, suppe, tunge

DIALECT MAPS are not just a way of presenting information that has been obtained by dialect surveys. In this unit, we see that they can also be used to tell us things about changes that have taken place or are taking place in the language.

Dialect map

Map 6.1, for example, shows the word for *play* as recorded by the SED. It can be seen that, in Traditional English Dialects, there are two different words. The word *play* is to be found in the south of England, as well as in Scotland and the far northeast of England. The word *laik*, on the other hand, is found in most of Cumbria, in parts of Northumberland and Durham, in Cleveland, North Yorkshire, northern Humberside, northern Lancashire, West Yorkshire, most of South Yorkshire, and parts of Greater Manchester, Derbyshire, Nottinghamshire and South Yorkshire. We know what the reason for this geographical distribution is. As any etymological dictionary will show, the word *laik* is Scandinavian in origin. (The word for 'to play' is *leike* in Modern Norwegian, and *leka* in Modern Swedish.) The geographical distribution of *laik* in northern England reflects to an extent the areas in which the Anglo-Saxon population was infiltrated or, in some areas, overwhelmed

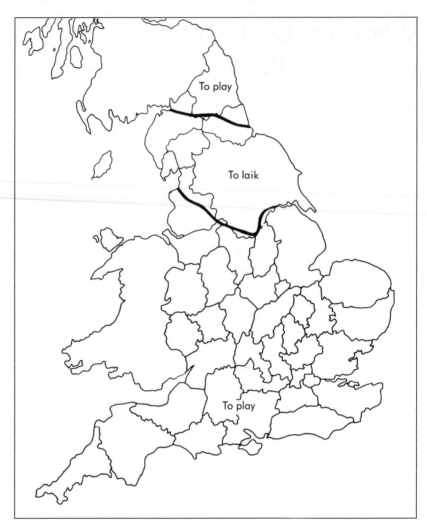

6.1
To play in
Traditional Dialects

by the invasion of the Vikings over a thousand years ago. Thus twenty-first-century dialects may still be able to tell us something about historical events even at some considerable time depth.

More recent linguistic events can sometimes be seen to be illustrated even more clearly in dialect maps. Map 6.2, for instance, deals with an accent feature, the pronunciation of words like *arm* and *four* which have an *r* in the spelling before another consonant or at the end of the word (we already mentioned this feature briefly in **Unit 4**). In some parts of the country, this *r* is not pronounced, so that arm sounds like **ahm** [aːm], four sounds like **faw** [fɔː], and *mar* and *Ma* are pronounced the same [maː], while in other parts of the country the *r* is pronounced – **arrm** [aːrm], **fourr** [fɔːr] – and *mar* and *Ma* are pronounced differently [maːr ~ maː]. It is very clear, just from looking at this map, that it is the **ahm**

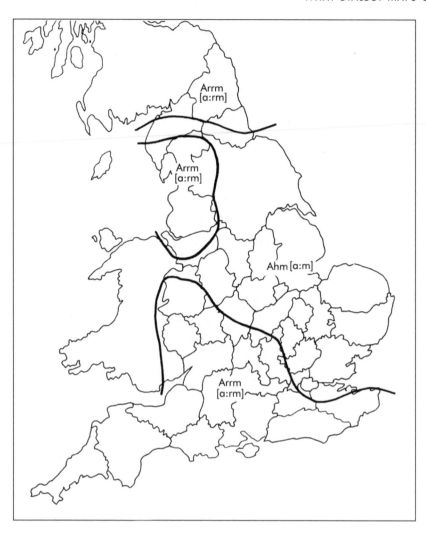

Arrm
[aːrm]

Arrm
[aːrm]

Ahm [aːm]

Arrm
[aːrm]

6.2
r in Traditional
Dialects

[aːm] pronunciation which is the newer of the two. That is, it is the loss of *r* which is an innovation, and not its introduction. This is rather obvious because there are three separate *r*-pronouncing **arrm** [aːrm] areas, and only a single *r*-less **ahm** [aːm] area. It is an obvious deduction that an innovation is very unlikely to have started in three different areas at once. Rather, we can deduce that the loss of *r* (which we believe actually began to take place in the 1700s) probably began life in south-eastern England, and then began to spread northwards and northwestwards, especially along the communications corridors between London and Birmingham, and between London and the North, driving wedges into and between *r*-pronouncing areas.

This is confirmed if we compare the Traditional Dialect *r*-map with Map 6.3, which examines the same accent feature, but this time in the

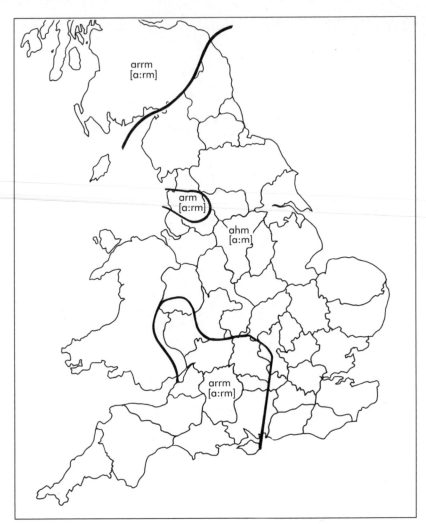

arrm
[aːrm]

arm
[aːrm]

ahm
[aːm]

arrm
[aːrm]

6.3
r in Mainstream
Dialects

Mainstream Dialects spoken by younger people, including those in urban areas. It can be seen that this *r* has disappeared completely from northeastern England, although it survives strongly in Scotland. It is also very much under threat in the northwest of England, where only a small area of Lancashire, in and around Blackburn, continues the older pronunciation. And the area of southern England where the **arrm** [aːrm] pronunciation survives has been forced back towards the west.

We can therefore use such dialect maps not only to tell us about the direction of change during previous generations. We can also use them to make predictions. The pronunciation of words like *arm* as **arrm** [aːrm], etc. will, we can suppose, very soon disappear from Kent, Surrey and Sussex altogether. Urban areas further west, such as Reading,

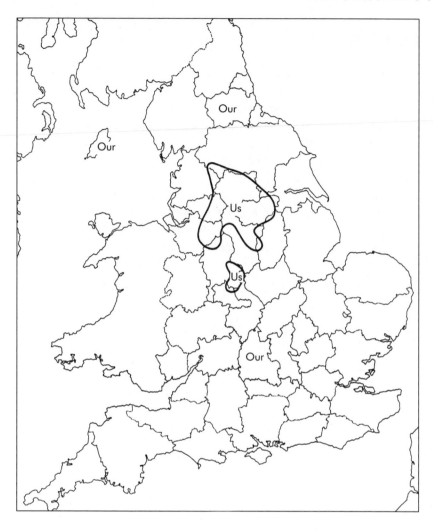

6.4
Our in Traditional Dialects

Southampton and Swindon, already show considerable signs of loss of *r*. In the speech of younger urban people, the **arrm** [aːrm] pronunciation is still strong in towns such as Gloucester, Bristol, Plymouth and Exeter. But it is quite likely that in a hundred years or so it will have disappeared from those areas too. If this does happen, the original pronunciation with *r* will survive only in Scotland and Ireland, in the British Isles. It will also, of course, survive in the United States and Canada, where the east-of-England-based innovation has never been so successful.

It is by no means certain, however, that the new form will actually continue to spread. As we shall see in the next unit, very often changes of this sort that are spreading geographically may come to a halt.

EXERCISES

6.1 Consider Map 6.4, which shows Traditional Dialect forms corresponding to Standard English *our*. You will see that there are two separate areas of northern England where dialect speakers generally say *We have us own food with us* rather than the *We have our own food with us* which is found in other parts of the country. Discuss why there are two separate *us* areas.

6.2 Consider Map 6.5, which shows the geographical distribution in Traditional Dialects of the words *married*, and *wedded* or *wed*. Consult an etymological dictionary for the origin of these words, and attempt an explanation for the geographical pattern portrayed in Map 6.5: why are the forms where they are?

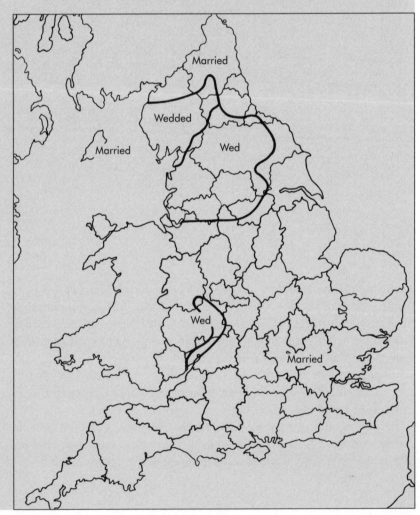

6.5
married in
Traditional
Dialects

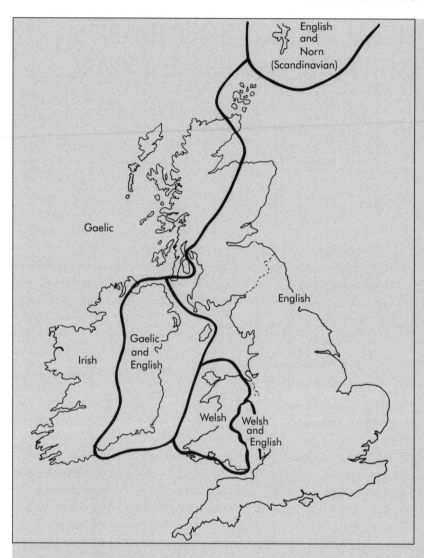

English
and
Norn
(Scandinavian)

Gaelic

English

Irish

Gaelic
and
English

Welsh

Welsh
and
English

6.6
Geographical
distribution of
speakers of
different languages
in the British Isles
(eighteenth century)

6.3 Consider Map 6.6, which shows the distribution of speakers of different languages in the British Isles in the eighteenth century. Discuss why these languages had this particular geographical distribution at that time.

6.4 Discuss why it is that, in many parts of the country, dialect words are dying out.

6.5 Think of twenty English words that you would guess are of French origin. Check in an etymological dictionary to see if you were correct.

7 HOW DIALECT BOUNDARIES GET TO BE WHERE THEY ARE

> Once we have drawn boundary lines between dialects on maps, we try to explain why they are where they are. The location of these lines may often be explained in terms of the spread of innovations from one area to another.

Some English words
fing, bruvver, bovver
nuffink, fistle, cloff

We saw in the previous unit that we can use dialect maps to draw historical conclusions about changes in the language. In this unit, we think further about geographical patterns, with particular reference to the explanation of why boundaries between dialect forms get to be where they are.

As we saw with some of the features we looked at in **Unit 6**, dialect boundaries lie at points where the geographical spread of new linguistic forms has come to a halt.

This geographical spreading of new words and pronunciations is not just something which happened in the past, though. A number of features of English can be observed to be spreading geographically in this way at the present time. Generally they spread along major lines of communication, and leap from one urban area to another before then spreading out into the surrounding countryside.

th-fronting   One accent feature which is behaving in this way in Britain at the moment is a phenomenon dialectologists call TH-FRONTING. We saw in **Unit 1** that **fing** [fɪŋ] is a typical Cockney pronunciation of *thing*. Since the 1970s, however, this pronunciation has been spreading geographically outwards from the London area. What is happening is this. There are two different **th** sounds in English. The first, [θ], is found in words like *thistle, thing, thought, ether* and *bath*. The second, [ð], is found in words like *this, there, them, other* and *bathe*. In *th*-fronting, the first **th** sound becomes merged with or replaced by **f**, while the second is merged with **v**. This means that, for example, *thought* is pronounced identically with *fought* [fɔːt], while *other* [ʌvə] rhymes with *cover* [kʌvə] (although words like *that, they* and *those*, with the second **th** sound [ð] at the beginning of the word, have not usually changed in the same way). This process is referred to as *fronting* because **f** and **v** are pronounced further forward in the mouth than **th** [θ ~ ð].

There is nothing very surprising about this sort of change, and nothing undesirable about it either. It is true that words which used to be pronounced differently are now pronounced the same, such as *thought* and *fought, thin* and *fin, thirst* and *first*. But the English language is perfectly capable of handling a loss of contrast of this sort. After all, if you heard someone described as being **tall and fin** [tɔːl n fɪn], it is very unlikely that you would believe that they were a fish. There are very many pairs of words that are pronounced the same in Modern English that used to be pronounced differently at earlier times, and nothing awful has happened to the language as a result of these changes. Pairs that used to be distinguished and no longer are include *knight* and *night, knave* and *nave, moan* and *mown, soul* and *sole, days* and *daze, maid* and *made, wrap* and *rap, wring* and *ring* – and hundreds more. There are even instances where four words that all used to be pronounced differently are now pronounced the same, such as *right, wright, rite* and *write*.

The interesting thing about the change from **th** to **f** and **v**, though, is the way in which we can watch it spreading across the country. In many parts of Britain, therefore, it is found in the speech of younger people but not older people. As a feature of younger people's speech, it appears, for instance, to have arrived in Norwich in the 1970s, Sheffield in the 1980s and Exeter in the 1990s. The last we heard, it had not yet arrived in Newcastle or Scotland.

Another accent feature which is spreading in a similar way is a new way of pronouncing **t**, except where it occurs at the beginning of a word. This new pronunciation, then, is not found in words like *tea* or *table*, but is found in *better* [bɛʔə], *bottle* [bɒʔl], *bat* [bæʔ] and *bought* [bɔːʔ]. It is sometimes referred to as 'dropping your *ts*', and shown in writing as *be'er*, etc. This is wrong. The *t* is not left out at all – if it was, *beating* [biːʔɪŋ] would sound the same as *being* [biːɪŋ], and *button* would sound the same as *bun*, which they don't. The *t* is still there, it is just pronounced without involving the tip of the tongue. Instead, it is pronounced as a GLOTTAL STOP. This is a sound which is produced in the larynx, by momentarily closing the vocal cords. It is a perfectly normal speech sound which occurs in many languages. In Danish, for instance, *mor* means 'mother' while *mo[ʔ]r* means 'murder'.

Glottal stop

Geographically, this new *t*-sound appears to have started about 150 years or so ago, perhaps in London. Since then it has spread across the country from place to place, arriving in urban areas first and then spreading out into neighbouring rural areas. At the moment pronunciations such as *better* [bɛʔə] are much more common in the south and east of Scotland and the eastern parts of England than it is in the Scottish Highlands, western England and Wales. It is clearly spreading, though, and is beginning to be common in Liverpool and Birmingham, and has very recently been introduced into Cardiff. In other parts of the country, though, a **d**-type pronunciation [bɛdə] may be used, or an **r** may be used in some words [bɛrə].

Another new pronunciation feature of dialects of English has to do with the way in which the consonant *l* is pronounced where it occurs after a vowel in words like *hill, heel, milk* and *bell*. It is very clear that this new pronunciation began in the London area. It involves the pronunciation of *l* as a vowel, rather like **oo**, so that *milk* is pronounced **miook** [mɪʊk], and *heel* **hee-oo** [hiːʊ] or **ee-oo** [iːʊ]. This change is spreading much less rapidly than the *th*-fronting change, but in many places within 100 miles of London, such as Cambridge and Oxford, this feature is much more common in the speech of younger people than it used to be.

EXERCISES

7.1 Discuss whether *th*-fronting has reached your area yet. Are there people in your area who say **fing** and **bruvver**? What sort of people are they? Are they mostly younger people, or do older people have this feature as well? If people in your group come from different areas of the country, compare notes and see if any definite geographical pattern emerges.

7.2 One of the consequences of the change in the pronunciation of *l* is that in quite a large area of the country certain vowels have very different pronunciations where they occur before *l* than they have elsewhere. Check your pronunciation, and that of other people in your group, to see if you can hear very big differences in the pronunciation of the vowels in the following pairs of words:

comb	coal
hose	whole
road	roll

rude	rule
mews	mule
food	fool

If your group consists of people from different areas, see if any geographical pattern emerges with respect to vowels before *l*.

7.3 A further development due to the change in pronunciation of *l* is that pairs of vowels that are otherwise distinct have come to be merged – to sound the same – where they occur before an *l*. Check whether the accents of people in your group have undergone any development in this direction by seeing if they pronounce any of these pairs of words the same:

dole	doll
fill	feel
pull	pool
Paul	pole
pull	Paul
Paul	pool
pal	pale

7.4 Consider whether people in your area use glottal stops as a way of pronouncing *t*. Say out loud *He's got a lot of little bottles*. Do you use glottal stops in *got, lot, little* and *bottles*? Do you use no glottal stops at all? Do you use a **d**-sound in some of these words? Or do you say **gorra** and **lorra** for *got a* and *lot of*? Does any geographical pattern emerge from a comparison of different speakers in your group?

8

SPOT YOUR DIALECT AREA

English dialects differ from one another in all sorts of ways. In this section we list some of the main pronunciation differences that are associated with the different regions of Britain.

Some words that are pronounced the same in Norfolk

feud	food
here	hair
moon	moan
purr	pure
bear	beer

One of the tasks that dialectologists often set themselves is the construction of overall dialect maps which deal not with individual words or pronunciations, but with the dialects of a country as a whole. In this unit, we examine in an introductory kind of way how we might draw a map for England that would give us a picture of the division of the country into its major accent areas as far as Mainstream Dialects of English are concerned.

In order to make this division, we have to select a number of pronunciation criteria that we believe to be important and that will give us a reasonably accurate picture of regional differences within the area in question. The features we have selected for this purpose are the following.

1 *ARM AS AHM* [aːm] **OR** *ARRM* [aːrm] (see Unit 6)

As we saw in **Unit 6**, **arrm** is the older pronunciation, and the loss of **r** which seems to have started in the southeast of England has not yet reached western areas. There are two major areas (see Map 6.3) which retain the older **arrm** pronunciation. The first consists of Devon and Cornwall, including the towns of Exeter, Plymouth, Truro and Penzance, as well as Somerset, Avon, Dorset, Wiltshire, Gloucestershire, Oxfordshire, Herefordshire, Shropshire (except for the north and extreme east), the far south of Worcestershire and Warwickshire, Berkshire, western Buckinghamshire, Northamptonshire (the southwestern part) and Hampshire. The second area consists of Scotland.

2   *HILL* AS *HILL* [hɪl] **OR** *ILL* [ɪl] (see Unit 4)

As we saw in **Unit 4**, this consonant has been lost in most local accents in England and Wales. It still survives very strongly in Ireland, and is only now on the point of disappearing in rural East Anglia. But the only part of Britain where all local dialect speakers still retain the older pronunciation is Scotland, together with the northeast of England – this area includes towns such as Berwick, Newcastle, Gateshead, Sunderland and Hartlepool, and is made up of the counties of Northumberland, Durham, Tyne and Wear, and eastern Cumbria and northern Cleveland.

There is, of course, nothing praiseworthy about the retention of the original pronunciation in the Northeast, nor is there anything to condemn in the loss of **h** in the other dialects. Many consonants have been lost and gained during the development of the English language, and the language survives regardless. For example, the fact that we now pronounce *knit* **nit** [nɪt] rather than the original **k-nit** [knɪt] doesn't cause any problems and doesn't appear to trouble anybody unduly.

3   *BUT* AS *BOOTT*, SO THAT IT RHYMES WITH *PUT*, OR AS *BUTT*, SO THAT IT DOES NOT (see Unit 4)

This feature is, of course, one of the best known of all features which distinguish between the accents of England – most people are aware that northerners say **boott** [bʊt] and southerners say **butt** [bʌt]. The reason for the difference is that the northern pronunciation is the original form. The new pronunciation of *but* [bʌt], *up*, *other*, etc., with a vowel different from the vowel in *put* [pʊt], *pull*, *butcher*, etc., is an innovation which started life in southern England several hundred years ago and never spread to the Midlands or the North. The result is that southern accents have one more vowel than northern accents.

The northern area with the original **boott** [bʊt] pronunciation includes Newcastle, Sunderland, Hartlepool, Carlisle, Lancaster, Liverpool, Manchester, Chester, Wrexham, Derby, Birmingham, Nottingham,

Leicester, Lincoln, Grantham and Peterborough. It covers Northumberland, Durham, Tyne and Wear, Cumbria, Cleveland, Merseyside, Greater Manchester, Cheshire (with neighbouring areas of Wales), Staffordshire, West Midlands (with neighbouring areas of Warwickshire and Worcestershire), northern Shropshire, Derbyshire, Nottinghamshire, Leicestershire and most of Lincolnshire. The southern area with the newer **butt** [bʌt] pronunciation includes Wales (except the northeast), southern Shropshire, Herefordshire, Gloucestershire, southern Worcestershire and Warwickshire, southern and eastern Northamptonshire, Cambridgeshire (except Peterborough), Norfolk and all areas to the south. It includes Shrewsbury, Hereford, Cheltenham, Oxford, Huntingdon, Bedford, Northampton, Cambridge and Norwich. Scotland, together with the town of Berwick in northern Northumberland, also has the newer pronunciation. (Why Scotland and southern England agree on this feature and differ from the intervening area of northern England, we do not know.)

4 LONG AS LONG [lɒŋ] OR LONGG [lɒŋg]

In most dialects of English, in the British Isles and overseas, the *g* in words such as *long* is not pronounced anymore, and *winger* and *finger* do not rhyme. In one area of England, however, the original pronunciation is still used – the *g* is pronounced so that the hard **g** of *give* can be heard at the end of words like *long* and *thing* [θɪŋg]. This area includes Liverpool, Manchester, Chester, Derby and Birmingham. It covers Merseyside, Greater Manchester, Cheshire, Staffordshire, West Midlands (with neighbouring areas of Warwickshire and Worcestershire), northern Shropshire and Derbyshire.

5 FACE AS FAYCE [fɛɪs] OR FEHCE/FAIRCE [fɛːs]

The long **a** vowel used to be a pure vowel or monophthong in all dialects of English. During the last 200 years or so, though, starting in the south-east of England, it has begun to turn into a DIPHTHONG – a vowel which changes its quality during its pronunciation – **eh-ee** [ɛɪ] or **a-ee** [æɪ]. From there, it has spread northwards and westwards, but it has not yet reached the north of England or the far Southwest. The older pronunciation is thus **fehce** or **fairce** [fɛːs] (with a vowel similar to that in BBC English **fair**), while the newer pronunciation we can write **fayce**.

Because of the way this change has spread outwards from the Southeast, there are today three separate areas with the older pure monophthongal **fehce** [fɛːs] pronunciation. The first is a large area which

Diphthong

takes in Scotland, Cumbria, Northumberland, Durham, Cleveland, North Yorkshire, West Yorkshire, South Yorkshire, Lancashire and Humberside, and includes the towns of Aberdeen, Edinburgh, Glasgow, Sunderland, Middlesborough, Carlisle, Lancaster, Leeds, Halifax, Huddersfield, Bradford, York, Blackburn and Hull. The second is Wales. And the third is the only area of southern England which has not yet acquired the newer **fayce** [fɛɪs] pronunciation, which is not surprising in view of this area's geographical distance from London, and consists of the counties of Devon and Cornwall.

These five features can be used to divide Britain up into nine major areas (see **Exercise 8.1**). It is important to note three points here, however. First, these areas do have many differences within them – the dialect of Newcastle is clearly by no means identical with the dialect of Hartlepool, for example, even though they come into the same area. People from Aberdeen sound very different from people from Glasgow. And the dialect of Dover is obviously rather different from the dialect of Northampton. If we had the time and space, we could make many more subdivisions.

Second, the different major DIALECT AREAS often merge into one another rather than being abruptly distinct. Any lines on a map are there- **Dialect area** fore suggestive rather than marking clear boundaries.

Third, because, as we have seen earlier, accent differences are related to social background as well as to geographical area, by no means every- body who comes from a particular area will have all the typical pronunci- ations – this will often be true of only the *most* local of local accents.

EXERCISES

8.1 Take a map of Britain and draw lines on it separating areas which have one variant of each of the five features from areas which have the other variant. You should have:

> lines separating the two **arrm** [aːrm] areas from the **ahm** [aːm] area;
>
> a line separating the **hill** [hɪl] area from the **ill** [ɪl] area;
>
> a line separating the **butt** [bʌt] area from the **boott** [bʊt] area;
>
> a line separating the **longg** [lɒŋɡ] area from the **long** [lɒŋ] area;
>
> and lines separating the three **fehce** [fɛːs] areas from the **fayce** [fɛɪs] area.

This should give you a map with nine main dialect areas. Label these areas on the map, as appropriate, with one of the following names:

> Scotland, The Northeast, The North, Wales, The West Central Area, The East Central Area, The Western Southwest, The Eastern Southwest, The Southeast.

8.2 For each of the nine areas, list which variant of each of the five pronunciation features is typical.

8.3 For each of our five accent features there is an original and a newer variant:

	Original		Newer	
arm	**arrm**	[aːrm]	**ahm**	[aːm]
hill	**hill**	[hɪl]	**ill**	[ɪl]
but	**boott**	[bʊt]	**butt**	[bʌt]
long	**longg**	[lɒŋg]	**long**	[lɒŋ]
face	**fehce**	[fɛːs]	**fayce**	[fɛɪs]

For each of the nine dialect areas, count how many original and newer pronunciations each area has. Which area has the most newer forms? Which area has the most original pronunciations? Which areas are intermediate? Why do you suppose this is?

8.4 Look at the spellings and rhymes in the following pieces of doggerel, and work out as precisely as you can, on the basis of the pronunciation evidence, which dialect areas they represent.

(a) Young 'Arry, 'e tried just as 'ard as 'e could,
But 'e just couldn't 'elp getting covered in mud.

(b) The Guy Fawkes display caused a great deal of anger
On the part of the man who got hit by a banger.

(c) If I had the money to travel to China,
I'd go in a plane and not in a liner.

8.5 Make a short list of other regional pronunciation features, in addition to the five we discussed above, that you could use in helping you to decide where a speaker comes from.

8.6 Whichever of the regions we have just discussed that you live in or come from, discuss differences of pronunciation that you are aware of *within* that region.

8.7 Discuss how far you have to travel from where you live before you start noticing that people speak differently.

PRESENT-TENSE VERBS

9

English dialects differ from each other in their grammatical structures as well as their pronunciation. In this section we exemplify this by examining how different dialects construct present-tense verb forms.

A passage from the Bible

Thou art the Lord. Thou hast made heaven, the earth, the seas and all that is in them, and thou preservest all of them. Thou art the Lord who didst choose Abram. And thou hast fulfilled thy promise, for thou art righteous.

Many people think that nonstandard dialects of English are 'ungrammatical', that they 'don't have grammar' or that their grammar is in some way 'wrong'. As we saw in **Unit 1**, beliefs such as these are quite wrong. Just as all languages have grammar, so all dialects – of English or any other language – have grammar. In this unit we show that the grammar of the nonstandard dialects of English differs from that of Standard English at a number of points, just as the grammar of English differs from that of French, but that these nonstandard dialects are simply grammatically *different* from Standard English, not *defective* in any way.

One of the things that the dialectologist of English has to do is to investigate and describe the grammar of the nonstandard dialects, and see how they differ from one part of the country to another, or from one social group to another. The Standard English dialect of England and Wales has been investigated by large numbers of grammarians and described in lots of grammar books. This is why it's often convenient to describe the grammar of English nonstandard dialects by comparing them to Standard English. What dialectologists are really trying to do, though, is to analyse the grammar of these dialects in their own right.

Dialectologists look for the systems and regularities and grammatical rules that are typical of the particular dialect they happen to be investigating.

For example, foreigners studying English are taught that present-tense verbs in Standard English have the following sorts of forms:

	Singular		Plural
1st person	I *sing*		we *sing*
2nd person		you *sing*	
3rd person	he/she/it *sings*		they *sing*

Person (PERSON is a term for the distinction between *I* or *we*, *you* and all other forms.) The rule that they have to learn is that present-tense verbs don't take any ending except in the third-person singular, where they take the ending *-s*. So verbs with subjects like *he*, *she*, *it*, *the girl*, *the short policeman* and *the grey thatched cottage* take the *-s* ending, while first- and second-person, and third-person plural verbs with subjects like *I*, *we*, *the young men*, and *you boys* don't have a following *-s*.

It interests dialectologists, though, that lots of nonstandard dialects of English have grammatical structures which are not the same as Standard English at this point. If you look at the following passage, which is written in the dialect of Norwich, you will see that it has a different kind of grammatical pattern.

> Every time they go round John's, there's trouble. He like his peace and quiet, and I understand that, but they don't see it at all. They get cross with him, and he get cross with them – you know how that is – and everybody end up shouting. Whenever we say anything about it, though, he don't like that neither.

As you can tell, East Anglian verb forms don't have a present-tense ending at all, in any person. The pattern is:

	Singular		Plural
1st person	I *sing*		we *sing*
2nd person		you *sing*	
3rd person	he/she/it *sing*		they *sing*

This same rule for present-tense verbs is used in most East Anglian (Norfolk and Suffolk) dialects. It is also found in a number of (particularly Black) American dialects, and in many dialects of Caribbean English.

A different rule for the formation of present-tense verbs is illustrated in the next passage, which is written in the traditional dialect of Berkshire.

I sees him every day on my way home. He likes to stop and have a chat, and I generally has the time for that. We often stops in at that pub – you goes there sometimes too, right? – and he has plenty of friends there and they often buys us a drink.

The grammatical rule for present-tense verb forms in the Berkshire dialect is obviously not the same as the one in Standard English. As you can see, Berkshire verb forms have the present-tense -s for *all* persons. The verbs go like this:

	Singular		Plural
1st person	I sings		we sings
2nd person		you sings	
3rd person	he/she/it sings		they sings

Present-tense verb forms like this are part of the grammatical structure of dialects in many areas of southwestern England and South Wales, as well as other areas.

These dialects, like all other dialects, have rules about the way their present-tense verb systems work. These systems are different from one another, but none of them is more or less systematic or grammatical than any other. Grammar varies from place to place, just as it varies from time to time. In fifteenth-century English, for instance, present-tense verb forms in the London area worked like this:

	Singular	Plural
1st person	I sing	we sing
2nd person	thou singest	you sing
3rd person	he/she/it singeth	they sing

and in the fourteenth century they worked like this:

	Singular	Plural
1st person	I singe	we singen
2nd person	thou singest	ye singen
3rd person	he/she/it singeth	they singen

Modern English is neither better nor worse than the older stages of the language in terms of linguistic structures, and the same is just as true of the different dialects of Modern English. They all have grammar. It's just that their grammar is different.

EXERCISES

9.1 Translate the following passage into (a) East Anglian dialect; and (b) Berkshire dialect, using appropriate present-tense verb forms:

> Richard knows a lot about places to go to, but I study more than he does, and we see very little of each other now. My other friends seem not to be very good at going out either. We get together sometimes, but you know how it is – when you have work to do, you have to do it (even if Richard doesn't!).

9.2 Consider the following passage, which is written in the older London Cockney dialect, and see if you can analyse what grammatical rule for present-tense verbs is in operation here. The rule exemplified is rather more complex than those for East Anglia and Berkshire illustrated above. The problem is to account for the use of forms such as *I stop* as well as *I says*, and (*they*) *stand* as well as (*they*) *comes*.

> I generally stop and have a word with him when we meet in the street, and he always seems pleased to meet me. But the other day, over by them trees that stand by the shops, he comes up to me and starts shouting. And all the people comes out of the shops and stares at us and I says to him 'I don't know what you mean' and I walks off right quick. He was drunk, you see. I expect when I see him tomorrow, he'll have forgotten all about it.

9.3 Consider the third-person singular present-tense verb forms in the following Shakespearean sonnet, and try to explain why Shakespeare uses the forms that he does.

> When I consider every thing that grows
> Holds in perfection but a little moment;
> That this huge stage presenteth nought but shows
> Whereon the stars in secret influence comment;
> When I perceive that men as plants increase,
> Cheered and check'd even by the self-same sky,
> Vaunt in their youthful sap, at height decrease,
> And wear their brave state out of memory:
> Then the conceit of this inconstant stay
> Sets you most rich in youth before my sight,
> Where wasteful Time debateth with Decay
> To change your day of youth to sullied night,

> And all in war with Time for love of you,
> As he takes from you, I ingraft you new.

9.4 Consider how present-tense verb forms work in languages you know other than English, with particular reference to pronunciation rather than spelling, and note what differences there are in the distinctions made between these languages and different English dialects.

9.5 Discuss how people in your area set about telling stories and jokes: how they begin, what sorts of verb forms they use, how they end stories, and so on. If people in your group come from different areas, compare notes, and see if there are any regional differences to be noted.

10 DIFFERENT DIALECTS, DIFFERENT GRAMMAR

> Some dialects have grammatical distinctions and use grammatical categories that are not found in other dialects. Some nonstandard English categories are lacking from Standard English, and vice versa.

A passage in Somerset dialect

It was like this in them days, years ago. A lot of the villagers did rent this land, this peat land, did rent a plot, half an acre, for ten year, for to excavate it. All as their fire stuff did cost them then, you see, in the home was their labour.

In this unit, we make the point that there isn't always a straightforward one-to-one relationship between the grammars of different dialects. The dialectologist, in other words, can't always simply work out which form in one dialect corresponds to which form in another dialect. The point is that dialects may differ from one another in the grammatical devices they have, and in the grammatical distinctions they are able to make. Sometimes a single form in one dialect may correspond to two or more forms in another, because the second dialect makes a grammatical distinction which the first one doesn't make. As we saw in **Unit 9**, Standard English makes a grammatical distinction between third-person singular verb forms and the other persons which the East Anglian and Berkshire dialects don't make. Similarly, the Cockney dialect has a distinction between narrative verb forms and other verb forms which Standard English doesn't have.

The situation in the Traditional Dialects of Berkshire and elsewhere in the west of England and South Wales, in fact, is actually rather more complicated than we suggested in **Unit 9**. It is true, as we saw, that the Berkshire dialect has the *-s* ending for all persons on present-tense verbs.

But this dialect also makes a grammatical distinction with present-tense verb forms which isn't made in Standard English.

To work out what this distinction is, we need to note that there are actually two verbs *to do* and two verbs *to have* in English. First, both *do* and *have* are full verbs which have complete meanings, such as *to do* = 'to make, to perform, to indulge in', etc. and *to have* = 'to possess, to own, to consume', etc. In sentences such as the following, *do* and *have* are full verbs:

> They do their homework when they get home.
> He does lots of useful things in the village.
> We always do the best we can.
>
> I have my tea at five o'clock.
> I have three sisters and two brothers.
> He has many such opportunities.

Second, *to do* and *to have* are also AUXILIARY or grammatical verbs which have nothing to do with 'doing' or 'having' but are used instead to do different grammatical tasks in English. In the case of *to do*, these include the formation of questions and negatives:

Auxiliary

> Do you come here often?
> I don't like it all.
> You don't want any, do you?

In the case of *to have*, the grammatical task is the formation of 'perfect-tense' forms:

> I have made several of them.
> Have you finished it yet?
> I've got lots of those.

Bearing in mind this distinction between full verbs and auxiliaries, look at the following passage in Berkshire dialect. You will be able to see both the occurrence of present-tense forms of *to do* and *to have* without -*s* (*do, don't, have, 've*) *and* present-tense forms of *to do* and *to have* with the -*s* ending (*dos* – pronounced to rhyme with *lose* – and *has*).

> Yes, we often has a drink in there, but I haven't got a lot of money,
> and I has to be careful about how much I spends. They don't pay
> much at my sort of work at the moment, though I dos a lot of overtime
> when I gets the chance. Do you find you has much left over these

days? – you always have worked as many hours as you could.
But there don't seem to be a lot to show for it, do there? Well, I'd
better be off. My children always has their meal about now, and they
haven't got much patience when it comes to waiting for me. My wife
dos the best she can, but she has a job on her hands with my
daughter – we've got a right one there!

Obviously, the correct explanation for why the Berkshire dialect has these different grammatical forms can't be to do with singular versus plural forms or with first-person versus second-person and/or third-person. All persons show forms both with and without -s, e.g.:

I haven't got	vs	I has to be
Do there?	vs	my wife dos
they haven't got	vs	my children has

In fact, the correct explanation is that in this dialect present-tense -s occurs for all persons for all verbs *except* auxiliary *do* and auxiliary *have*, which do not take -s in any person. (While the full verb form of *to do* is *dos*, the corresponding form of *to have* is not **haves* but *has*.)

Bearing in mind the distinction we have just introduced between auxiliary and full verbs, now see what *past*-tense forms of *to do* turn up in the following passage, written in a nonstandard dialect of English.

You done plenty of that in your time, didn't you? I wouldn't have done
it myself, but my sister done the same sort of work, and she never did
regret it. What did you think when you heard about it? I bet you
didn't think it was him what done it.

You were probably able to work out that the grammatical rule here is that the past tense of the full verb *to do* is *done*, while the past tense of the auxiliary verb is *did*. (Standard English has *did* in both cases.) This rule for the past tense of *do* occurs not just in Berkshire but in most nonstandard dialects of English around the world – in the United States, Australia and elsewhere – as well as in the British Isles. Standard English is the odd dialect out, since it's the only one which doesn't make this grammatical difference between auxiliary *did* and full verb *done*.

EXERCISES

10.1 Translate the following Standard English passage into the traditional Berkshire dialect, assigning present-tense -*s* endings according to the rule discussed above:

> My husband and I have a number of different properties. We do our best to maintain them all. We don't always succeed and we have often had problems, but on the whole I have to admit that we do very well. Do you own a weekend place yourself? My husband does much of the gardening, but I do the painting, and we also have to do quite a lot of the general maintenance. Every time we go over to France, we find something that has to be done. We have been very fortunate, mostly, though.

10.2 Which of the following sentences are ungrammatical in all dialects of English? Which of them are ungrammatical only in Standard English?

(a) You done it, did you?

(b) Done she see it?

(c) I did it yesterday.

(d) They did it, done they?

(e) What did they do?

(f) She did it, did she?

(g) Did you have any luck?

(h) I didn't see any.

(i) Where done they go?

(j) They done it last year.

10.3 Here are some sentences in Somerset dialect. Work out what the rule is for using the two different types of past-tense verb forms.

> I did go there every day.
> I went there last night.
> I seen 'im last Thursday.
> I did see 'im regular.
> I told 'er as soon as I could.
> I did tell 'er every time it happened.
> We always did have a cup of tea at four o'clock.
> We had a cup of tea just now.

We did play football when we was kids.
We played football yesterday afternoon.

10.4 Here are some sentences in East Anglian dialect, with impossible sentences indicated by *. Work out what the rules are in this dialect for the use of *that* and *it*.

* It's raining.
That's no good, is it?
* It's a bit windy.
I don't want it.
That's cold in here.
* It's very nice.
* That's no good, is that?
That's raining.
* It's no good, is it?
That's very good.
That's a bit windy.
I can't get on with it.

10.5 The verb *must* is used in two different ways in English, as in:

You must take these pills twice a day.

and

You must be feeling very cold.

First, work out what the difference in meaning is between these two different usages. Second, work out what the *negative* forms of these sentences would be in your own dialect, introducing *not* or *n't* into the sentences. Broadly speaking, in the south of England, the two different meanings take two different negative forms, while in the north of England, and Scotland, only one negative form is found.

10.6 Discuss what *You haven't got to do that* means in your dialect. In some parts of Britain it can only mean 'It is not compulsory or necessary for you to do that', whereas in other parts of the country, particularly in the north of England, it can mean, as well or instead, 'You must not do that – it is compulsory for you not to do that'.

10.7 Make a list of grammatical differences between Standard English and the local dialect in your own region or regions. You might like to consider the following possibilities:

The past-tense forms of irregular verbs, e.g. *gave, came, saw, did.*

The plural demonstrative form *those.*

Present-tense verb forms, e.g. *I go, she goes.*

Reflexive pronouns, e.g. *himself, themselves.*

Negative sentences, e.g. *He doesn't want any.*

Relative pronouns, e.g. *Are you the person who did it?*

10.8 The Traditional Dialects of parts of southwestern England such as Somerset used to have an interesting system of third-person singular pronouns. This system has now broken down somewhat, but is still retained in some of the Traditional Dialects of Newfoundland which are derived from dialects of southwestern England. Here is a list of nouns and their corresponding pronouns, which is intended to indicate that sentences such as *Pass me the hammer – he's on that bench* would be normal in the dialect. See if you can work out how this system of pronouns works.

hammer	he	love	it
sugar	it	milk	it
boat	she	raincoat	he
boy	he	rain-shower	she
cow	she	brother	he
salt	it	mother	she
loaf	he	soldier	he
car	she	truck	she
man	he	table	he
girl	she	cheese	it
mare	she	salt	it
bull	he	peace	it
plane	she	piece	he
book	he	snow	it
bread	it	knife	he
stallion	he	ewe	she
beauty	it	truth	it
stone	he	sugar	it
rain	it	pen	he
wind	she	water	it

11 DIALECT GRAMMAR – THE OLD AND THE NEW

> Many grammatical differences between English dialects are due to the fact that changes that have taken place in some dialects have not taken place in others. In some respects Standard English is more innovative than other dialects, in others more conservative.

Some British English verb forms

burnt	dreamt	learnt	leant
smelt	spilt	spoilt	knelt

Some American English verb forms

burned	dreamed	learned	leaned
smelled	spilled	spoiled	kneeled

How do different dialects get to have different grammatical structures? The short answer to this is that, just as with accent differences, differences are the result of LINGUISTIC CHANGE. We have to admit that we don't really know why languages change, but we know that all human languages do change, and that they change in different ways in different places and at different times. If Standard English has grammatical differences from the other, nonstandard dialects of English, this must be either because Standard English has gone through changes that the other dialects haven't gone through, or vice versa.

It would not be true to say that Standard English is more conservative than the nonstandard dialects. At some points it is clearly innovative. Most dialects of English, for example, continue to allow multiple negation ('double negatives') to occur in sentences, like earlier stages of the English language. Standard English, on the other hand, has lost the ability to do this, so that:

Linguistic change

I couldn't see none nowhere.

is grammatical in most dialects of English, but isn't grammatical in Standard English, which would have instead the newer form

I couldn't see any anywhere.

In other cases, though, it is easy to see that it is the nonstandard dialects that are leading the way in linguistic change and that it is Standard English which is conservative. For example, one of the most important ways in which grammar can change is REGULARISATION. This means getting rid of irregularities in favour of patterns that are more regular and more common in the language. For instance, most verbs in the English language are REGULAR VERBS which have a pattern of present- and past-tense forms which, in Standard English, is like this:

Regularisation

Regular verb

Present tense	Past tense	Past participle
I *love*	I *loved*	I have *loved*
I *walk*	I *walked*	I have *walked*

The pattern in nonstandard dialects is the same or very similar. To form the past tense from the present tense, *-ed* or *-d* is added to the stem of the verb. The past participle – the part of the verb which goes together with *have* to produce perfect verb forms – is identical to the past-tense forms.

Many very common verbs in English, however, are so-called IR-REGULAR VERBS which differ from this regular pattern in a number of ways. First, the *-ed* ending isn't used; often, a change of vowel is used instead. Second, the past-tense form is often not identical to the past participle, so most of these verbs have three main forms rather than two. For example:

Irregular verb

Present tense	Past tense	Past participle
ring	rang	rung
see	saw	seen
come	came	come
write	wrote	written
know	knew	known

Some are even more irregular than this:

Present tense	Past tense	Past participle
go	went	gone
am	was	been

Over the centuries, a number of originally irregular verbs in English have become regular. It often happens during linguistic change that irregularities are levelled out in this way. After all, as you may know from learning a foreign language, irregular forms are much harder to learn and remember than regular ones. For instance, the forms of the verb *to help* used to be:

Present tense	Past tense	Past participle
help	holp	holpen

Now they are:

Present tense	Past tense	Past participle
help	helped	helped

This process of regularisation has often gone further in nonstandard dialects than in Standard English. Regularisation can take two forms. First, the number of forms involved can be reduced from three to two. We've already seen one example of this in **Unit 10**, in the case of the full lexical verb *to do*:

Standard English:	do	did	have done
Nonstandard English:	do	done	have done

Second, irregular verbs may become completely regular:

Standard English:	draw	drew	have drawn
Nonstandard English:	draw	drawed	have drawed

One day, Standard English may catch up with the other dialects in changing at least some verb forms in the same sort of way.

EXERCISES

11.1 The following are irregular verbs with three major forms in Standard English. What are their past-tense and past-participle forms in the nonstandard dialect of your own area or the nonstandard dialect you are otherwise most familiar with?

to see	to write	to fly	to take
to drive	to draw	to give	to swim
to sing	to bite		

11.2 In what way can the nonstandard dialect pronouns shown below be said to be more regular than their Standard English counterparts?

Nonstandard

I hurt myself.
You hurt yourself.
He hurt hisself.
She hurt herself.
We hurt ourselves.
You hurt yourselves.
They hurt theirselves.

Standard

I hurt myself.
You hurt yourself.
He hurt himself.
She hurt herself.
We hurt ourselves.
You hurt yourselves.
They hurt themselves.

11.3 In what respect can the dialects of East Anglia and Berkshire be said to be more regular than Standard English (see **Unit 9**)?

11.4 If these past-tense verb forms were to be regularised, what would the new regular forms be?

went, saw, knew, left, rode, wrote, told, gave, bought, brought

11.5 List some grammatical points where the local dialect of your region or regions is more regular than Standard English. You might like to consider the same grammatical points mentioned in connection with **Exercise 10.7**.

11.6 We have seen in this unit that grammatical differences between dialects are the results of changes in the language. Consider these examples from the English of Sir Thomas Malory (d.1471), convert them into Modern English, and attempt an analysis of the grammatical changes that have taken place to give the Modern English forms.

> In his dream him seemed that he saw a chair.
> He knew not where he was.
> I am come to mine end.
> What sawest thou there?
> Doubt ye not ye must be slain.
> All these been ladies for whom I have foughten.
> I give you warning that in no wise ye do battle.
> God hath sent me.
> And who that were not dead, they slew them for their
> riches.
> Him thought sin to throw away that sword.
> Do as well as thou mayest.

12 OVERDOING THINGS

Contact between speakers of different dialects can lead to the development of a number of interesting processes, including hyperadaptation, which involves speakers trying to adopt features from other dialects without being totally successful.

A number of interesting things happen in dialect-contact situations – in situations where people who speak different dialects come into contact and communicate with one another. Usually there is no *need* for us to modify the way we speak very much in order for someone who speaks a different dialect to understand us – most English dialects are not that different from one another. All the same, it is a matter of common observation that we often do this anyway. We are influenced by the way people around us talk. A British person who goes to America for six months may well come back sounding rather more American than when they went away.

This influence that speakers can have on other speakers must play an important role in the way dialect forms spread from one part of the country to another, as we discussed in **Units** 7 and **8**. It is not surprising that London pronunciations tend to spread to other areas, simply because there are lots of Londoners. A person from Cambridge, say, has a thousand times more chance of meeting, and being influenced by, a Londoner, than a Londoner has of meeting someone from Cambridge. This type of face-to-face influence is much more important than the influence of radio and television – people don't change the way they speak very much because of what they hear on the TV, because they don't talk to the TV – and even if they do it can't hear them!

In certain situations, this mutual influence of dialect speakers on one another can have interesting consequences. For instance, where new towns are established, such as Milton Keynes, which people come to live in from all different parts of the country, a whole new dialect may grow up which is a mixture of the different dialects which the incomers bring with them.

One of the most interesting things that happens as a result of contact between dialects, though, is what dialectologists call HYPERADAPTA-TION. This refers to cases where speakers try to modify their speech in the direction of a different dialect and get it wrong because they overdo it.

Hyperadaptation

A well-known example is what sometimes happens when people from the north of England move to the south. As we saw in **Unit 8**, speakers in the Northeast, the North, the West Central area and the East Central area have one vowel less than speakers in Scotland, Wales and the southern English dialect areas. Speakers in Scotland, Wales and the south of England have six short vowels in words such as:

pit	put
pet	but
pat	pot

Speakers in the north of England have only five:

pit	put, but
pet	pot
pat	

If English Northerners want to change to a southern way of speaking they therefore have to change the pronunciation of words like *but* from **boott** [bʊt] to **butt** [bʌt]. The problem is that, if they do this, they have to know, and to remember, *not* to change the pronunciation of words like *put* from **poott** [pʊt] to **putt** [pʌt], because all dialects of English say **poott** [pʊt]. This is rather difficult to do, because each word has to be learnt individually, and the spelling is no help:

put-words	*but-words*
put	but
full	dull
pull	hull
good	blood
wood	flood
push	rush

It is therefore not surprising that people from one of the four northern dialect regions living in the south can sometimes be heard to say words like *cushion* and *butcher* and *hook* with the wrong vowel. They have modified their accents in the direction of the accents of the people they live amongst, but they have got it wrong and overdone things by changing the pronunciation not only of words that are different in the two parts of the country but also the pronunciation of words that are the same and should not have been changed.

We can say that what happens in such dialect-contact situations is that speakers have made an incorrect analysis of the dialect they are being influenced by. One group of people who really ought to know better but can quite often be heard making faulty analyses of this type are actors. If you listen to the BBC radio programme *The Archers* you will hear plenty of instances of this kind of thing. Some of the characters have accents, typical of the Eastern Southwest area, in which *arm* is pronounced **arrm** rather than **ahm** and *car* **carr** [kaːr] rather than **cah** [kaː]. However, it is clear that some of the actors don't normally themselves have accents of this type because, in trying to speak in this way, they put in **r**s where they don't belong. Their own pronunciation of *arm* is **ahm**, but they change it to **arrm** when they are acting this particular part. This is OK. Unfortunately, they also sometimes change the pronunciation of words like *calm* from **cahm** [kaːm], which is correct, to **carrm** [kaːrm], which is not.

English pop and rock singers trying to imitate an American accent can sometimes be heard to do the same thing. There is an early Beatles track ('Till there was you'), for example, where Paul McCartney can be heard to sing the words *I never saw them at all*, pronouncing the word saw as **sawrr** [sɔːr] in an exaggerated and incorrect attempt to sound like an American.

Hyperadaptations of this sort can also occur in grammar. For example, it is quite natural in all dialects of English to say things like:

> John and me went to the party.
> Our mothers and us read the book.

Some people, however, believe that it is 'incorrect' to use forms like *me* and *us* as the subjects of verbs, and that it is 'better' to say:

> John and I went to the party.
> Our mothers and we read the book.

Over the years these pedants have made such a fuss about this that many people today try to avoid using expressions like *John and me* even where they are not in subject position. You therefore sometimes hear people use hypercorrect expressions such as:

> He gave it to John and I.
> a good relationship between we and our mothers

EXERCISES

12.1 The following sentences contain hyperadaptive forms. Identify the forms, and explain how they came about.

(a) Between you and I, I don't think he looks very well.

(b) She's a person whom I don't think will be very successful.

(c) They want five happles and three horanges.

(d) We were walking along the pathement.

(e) I feel badly about it.

12.2 Given what you know about differences between north and south of England pronunciation, what hyperadaptive pronunciation of the word *gasmask* might you expect some English northerners to come up with in trying to acquire a southern accent?

12.3 Given what you know about differences between American and British English pronunciation, what hyperadaptive pronunciation of the word *ready* might you expect some Americans to come up with in trying to imitate a British accent?

12.4 In the dialect of Bristol, many speakers pronounce words like *America, India, Sandra, area, pasta* as **America l, Indial, Sandral, areal, pastal**. Dialectologists believe that this may be due, originally, to a process of hyperadaptation. If this is correct, what exactly would have happened?

12.5 Listen to one episode of *The Archers* on BBC radio and make a note of instances of hyperadaptive *r*.

FURTHER READING

This book has only been able to scratch the surface of the subject of English dialects and dialectology in general. If you would like to know more about dialects of English, there are a number of books that you might like to consult. These include:

A. Hughes and P. Trudgill, *English Accents and Dialects: An Introduction to Regional and Social Varieties of British English*, 3rd edn (London: Edward Arnold, 1995).

D. Murison, *The Guid Scots Tongue* (Glasgow: Blackwood, 1977).

P. Trudgill, *The Dialects of England* (Oxford: Blackwell, 1999).

P. Trudgill (ed.), *Language in the British Isles* (Cambridge: Cambridge University Press, 1985).

P. Trudgill and J.K. Chambers (eds), *Dialects of English: Studies in Grammatical Variation* (London: Longman, 1991).

C. Upton, S. Sanderson and J. Widdowson, *Word Maps: A Dialect Atlas of England* (Edinburgh: Croom Helm, 1987).

M. Wakelin, *English Dialects: An Introduction* (London: Athlone, 1972).

J.C. Wells, *Accents of English*, 3 vols (Cambridge: Cambridge University Press, 1982).

If you would like to read further about dialectology in general, relevant books include:

J.K. Chambers and P. Trudgill, *Dialectology* (Cambridge: Cambridge University Press, 1998).

W.N. Francis, *Dialectology* (London: Longman, 1985).

K.M. Petyt, *The Study of Dialect* (London: Deutsch, 1978).

You can learn more about the use of phonetic symbols in the following books:

Peter Roach, *English Phonetics and Phonology*, 3rd edition (Cambridge: Cambridge University Press, 2000).
Peter Roach, *Phonetics* (Oxford: Oxford University Press, 2001).

ANSWERS TO EXERCISES

UNIT 1   STUDYING ENGLISH DIALECTS

1.1   The poem, called 'Wuid-reek' (wood-smoke), by Sydney Goodsir Smith, is written in Scots.

1.2   This passage is written in American English. Well-known American features include *around* = British *round*, *color* = *colour*, *apartment* = *flat*, *squad car* = *police car*, *elevator* = *lift*, and *odor* = *odour*.

1.3   This is taken from a song written about a hundred years ago in the Cockney (London) dialect. Well-known Cockney features include *town* **tahn** [taːn] and *down* **dahn** [daːn], as well as *think* **fink** [fɪŋk] (though see **Unit 7** on the spread of this feature).

1.4   *nervy* in American English means 'brave, having lots of nerve' whereas in Britain it means more or less the opposite – 'nervous'.

scrappy in American English means 'full of fight, liking a scrap' whereas in Britain it means something more like 'untidy, messy'.

pavement in American English refers to 'paved road, roadway' whereas in Britain it corresponds to American English *sidewalk* = 'streetside footpath', so that *No Cycling On Pavement* means exactly the opposite in the United States from what it means in Britain.

homely in American English means 'not very good looking' as applied to a person whereas in Britain it means 'domestic, home-loving'.

momentarily in American English can mean 'for a moment' whereas in Britain it can only mean 'in a moment'.

cheap in American English tends to mean 'shoddy, cheap and nasty' whereas in Britain it most often means simply 'inexpensive'.

UNIT 2 POSH AND LESS POSH DIALECTS

2.1 The normal social convention that we operate with in the English-speaking world is that writing, particularly writing intended for publication, should be done in Standard English. This book is no exception – it is written in Standard English. This, however, is a matter of social convention. There is nothing that you can say or write in Standard English that can't be said or written in other dialects. That's why we have written this paragraph in a nonstandard dialect, just to make the point.

2.2 (a) standard

(b) nonstandard

(c) nonstandard

(d) standard

(e) nonstandard

(f) standard

(g) standard

(h) nonstandard

(i) nonstandard

(j) standard

(k) standard

(l) nonstandard

2.5 (a) I don't want any of that.

(b) Those tapes aren't any good.

(c) He gave it to me last night.

(d) It wasn't John I saw.

(e) They did what they were supposed to.

(f) That's the one that I want.

(g) We always go there on Saturdays.

(h) You wrote that very quickly.

(i) It was him that told me.

(j) I know I shouldn't have gone.

2.6 (a) England

(b) United States, Canada, Australia

(c) Wales

(d) United States, Canada

(e) Scotland, Northern Ireland, United States, Canada

(f)   United States, Canada

(g)   Scotland, Northern Ireland

(h)   Ireland

UNIT 3   ENGLISH IN MANY SHAPES AND FORMS

3.1   One possible rendering would be:

Mum was a bit annoyed when she saw that I hadn't taken my dirty clothes out of the kitchen and put them in a better place, a job I'd promised her I'd get done before Dad came home from work.

3.2   *Nonstandard dialect features*
come home = Standard English *came home*
I done = Standard English *I did*
He wasn't very interesting neither = Standard English *either*

Informal style features
old man = more formal *Dad, father*
bushed = more formal *tired, exhausted*
telly = more formal *TV, television*

Register gaps
operator doctor = *surgeon*
the one in charge of hospitals = *Minister of Health*
       (or something similar)

3.3

(a)	Nonstandard	technical	formal
(b)	Standard	nontechnical	informal
(c)	Nonstandard	technical	informal
(d)	Standard	nontechnical	formal
(e)	Standard	technical	formal
(f)	Nonstandard	nontechnical	informal
(g)	Nonstandard	technical	formal
(h)	Standard	nontechnical	informal
(i)	Nonstandard	technical	formal
(j)	Standard	nontechnical	informal

UNIT 4 DIALECTS – THE OLD AND THE NEW

4.1 I expect you wonder why I haven't written lately. Well, Aunt Agatha has been spring-cleaning, and we have very nearly finished. She has got only one more place to do – it's outside (it's the coal shed). Grandad complains. He says you can't see any difference when it's done, except that you can't find anything. But he lends a hand. We all got ready, when Aunt Agatha found she'd lent her whitewash brush to Mrs W., so I had to go after it. Well, mate, she said to me 'Thank your Aunt Agatha for the use of the brush. I have got a new one now so I won't want to borrow or lend'. She gave me some peppermint sweets for Grandad. He complained. He says 'I don't want those things'.

4.2 A man can't eat his food for wondering whether it will be yes or no. Before long he doesn't rightly care which of them it is if only it would be one of the two and be done with it. And if there's a thing you're frightened of, and it's coming, and not coming, and never coming – man, do you know after a while you would be glad of it coming, you would even go half-way to meet it, just not to have it coming, and not coming.

4.3 steeith = staithe = jetty
neet = night
freeten = frighten
deil = devil
lang = long
sang =song
nowt = nothing
quairts = quarts

4.4 wold = old
hwome = home
doust = dust
vell = fallen

UNIT 6 WHAT DIALECT MAPS CAN TELL US

6.1 The most obvious explanation is that there used to be a single *us* area which was larger than it is today, and that the area is shrinking under the influence of the other dialects' (and the Standard English) form *our*. As the *our* form has spread, it has eaten into the original *us* area, and split it into two.

6.2 *Wed* is the Anglo-Saxon or Old English form. *Married* was introduced from Norman French (compare Modern French *marié*) and has spread across most of the country, but it has not yet reached the Traditional Dialects of certain geographically rather peripheral areas.

UNIT 8   SPOT YOUR DIALECT

8.2

Southeast	ahm	ill	butt	long	fayce
Eastern Southwest	arrm	ill	butt	long	fayce
Western Southwest	arrm	ill	butt	long	fehce
East Central	ahm	ill	boott	long	fayce
West Central	ahm	ill	boott	longg	fayce
Wales	ahm	ill	butt	long	fehce
North	ahm	ill	boott	long	fehce
Northeast	ahm	hill	boott	long	fehce
Scotland	arrm	hill	butt	long	fehce

8.3 The distribution of original and newer forms is as follows:

	Original	*Newer*
Southeast	0	5
Eastern Southwest	1	4
East Central	1	4
Wales	1	4
Western Southwest	2	3
West Central	2	3
North	2	3
Northeast	3	2
Scotland	3	2

In each case, the innovatory pronunciation has begun in the English Southeast, and then spread northwards and westwards, leaving areas furthest away from London with older pronunciations. This is probably because there are more people living in the southeast of England than the other areas. Since the geographical spread of changes takes place by passing from person to person, it is simply a matter of statistics that changes which start in the Southeast have a better chance of spreading than changes which start in other areas.

8.4 (a)   The pronunciations without **h** show that this cannot be from the Northeast. The rhyme of *could* [kʊd] and *mud* [mʊd] shows that it must therefore be from the North, the West Central or the East Central area.

(b)   The rhyme of *anger* and *banger* indicates the pronunciation **bangger** [bæŋgə], which means that this piece must come from the West Central area.

(c)   All we can say about this piece is that the rhyme of *China* with *liner* indicates the pronunciation **lina** [laɪnə] rather than **linerr** [laɪnər], which means that it comes from somewhere *other than* Scotland, the Eastern Southwest or the Western Southwest.

UNIT 9   PRESENT-TENSE VERBS

9.1 (a)   Richard know a lot about places to go to, but I study more than he do, and we see very little of each other now. My other friends seem not to be very good at going out either. We get together sometimes, but you know how it is – when you have work to do, you have to do it (even if Richard don't!).

(b)   Richard knows a lot about places to go to, but I studies more than he does, and we sees very little of each other now. My other friends seems not to be very good at going out either. We gets together sometimes, but you knows how it is – when you has work to do, you has to do it (even if Richard doesn't!).

9.2 This dialect follows the Standard English pattern (third-person singular -*s* only) except for NARRATIVE PRESENT-TENSE verbs, i.e. where the present tense is used to narrate past events. In these cases the same pattern is used as in the Berkshire dialect, i.e. -*s* for all persons. At this point, then, London dialect is grammatically richer than Standard English.

Narrative present tense

9.3 Shakespeare uses both verb forms in -*eth*, such as *presenteth* and *debateth*, and verb forms in -*s*, such as *grows*, *holds*, *sets*, and *takes*. At the time when Shakespeare was writing, usage was variable, with older southern forms in -*eth* giving way in the south of England to newer, originally northern forms in -*s*. This meant that Shakespeare could alternate to indicate stylistic differences (with -*eth* forms being rather more formal) or, as here, to meet the demands of poetic metre, with the -*s* forms generally having one syllable fewer than the -*eth* forms.

UNIT 10   DIFFERENT DIALECTS, DIFFERENT GRAMMAR

10.1   My husband and I *has* a number of different properties. We *dos* our best to maintain them all. We *don't* always succeed and we *have* often had problems, but on the whole I *has* to admit that we *dos* very well. *Do* you own a weekend place yourself? My husband *dos* much of the gardening, but I *dos* the painting, and we also *has* to do quite a lot of the general maintenance. Every time we *goes* over to France, we *finds* something that *has* to be done. We *have* been very fortunate mostly, though.

10.2   Ungrammatical in all dialects of English:

(b) *Done she see it?

(d) *They did it, done they?

(i)   *Where done they go?

Ungrammatical in Standard English only:

(a) You done it, did you?

(j)   They done it last year.

10.3   There is a grammatical distinction in the Somerset dialect whereby single events are expressed through simple verb forms such as *go*, while habitual or repeated events are expressed through verb forms using auxiliary *do*, such as *did go*.

10.4   The rule is that the third-person singular neuter pronoun is always *it* when it is the object of a verb or preposition. When it is a grammatical subject, it is *that*, unless it is in unstressed position, where it is *it*.

10.5   The first meaning of *must* has to do with compulsion or obligation. The second meaning has to do with the speaker drawing conclusions from available evidence – 'You must be feeling very cold – because you are shivering.' Southern English dialects have two different negative forms, one with *mustn't* and the other with *can't*: *You mustn't take these pills* and *You can't be feeling very cold [because it's very warm in here].* Northern dialects use *mustn't* in both cases.

Mass noun

10.8   The solution to this problem is as follows. In this dialect, only MASS NOUNS take the pronoun *it*. Mass (or *noncount*) nouns are nouns like *bread*, *water*, *music* which refer to substances rather than things, which can't be counted (you can't say **three musics* in English), and which can't occur with the indefinite article – **a music* is not possible. All other nouns – count nouns – take either *he* or *she*. Animate nouns take *he* if they refer to masculine beings (*boy*, *stallion*) and *she* if they refer to feminine beings (*mother*, *ewe*). Inanimate count nouns take *he* unless they refer to 'self-moving' phenomena such as vehicles (*truck*) or natural phenomena (*rain-shower*). Thus *rain* is *it* (mass noun), *rain-shower* is *she* (count noun, self-moving), and *raincoat* is *he* (count noun, not self-moving).

UNIT 11 DIALECT GRAMMAR – THE OLD AND THE NEW

11.1 Although this list is not exhaustive, and you may have come up with other forms, possible nonstandard forms include the following:

	Past tense	*Past participle*
see	see/seen	–
write	writ	writ
fly	–	flew
take	–	took
drive	driv	drove/driv
draw	drawed	drawed/drew
give	give	give
swim	swum	swam
sing	sung	sang
bite	–	bit

11.2 The nonstandard dialect forms are all based on possessive pronouns plus *self* or *selves*: *my, your, his, her, our* and *their*. Some of the Standard English forms are based on possessive pronouns (*my, your, her, our*) while others are not (*him, them*).

11.3 Standard English is irregular in having present-tense -*s* only in the third-person singular. East Anglian and Berkshire dialects are more regular in having the same form for all persons.

11.4 goed, seed, knowed, leaved, rided, writed, telled, gived, buyed, bringed

UNIT 12 OVERDOING THINGS

12.1 (a) *Between you and I* is the indirect, hyperadaptive result of attempts to avoid forms of the type *John and me went*, mentioned above (page 62).

(b) The hyperadaptive form is *whom*, used here instead of *who*. Most English speakers no longer naturally make a distinction between the subject form *who* and the object form *whom*. However, attempts to argue that it is 'better' to use the older form *the man whom I saw* rather than the newer form *the man who I saw* have led some people who are trying to 'improve' their language to use *whom* even where it does not belong.

(c)   The hyperadaptive forms are, of course, *happle* and *horange*. Since the high-prestige BBC accent preserves the pronunciation of **h** in words like *hammer* and *house*, while local accents in most of England and Wales have lost it, people sometimes try to speak in a posher way by changing, not only **ammer** [æmə] to **hammer** [hæmə] but also **apple** [æpl] to **happle** [hæpl].

(d)   Some speakers who have this feature try to get rid of the *th*-fronting (see **Unit** 7) that is part of their natural accents and change **f** and **v** to **th** not only where this would be appropriate, as in words like *thing* and *this* but also where it is not appropriate, as in *pavement*.

(e)   Many nonstandard dialects do not distinguish between adjectival forms such as *quick* and adverbial forms such as *quickly*, e.g. *He runs very quick.* People not having the Standard English distinction in their own dialect and trying to convert nonstandard to standard forms may believe that, because *feel* is a verb, it ought to be qualified by an overtly adverbial form such as *badly* rather than an adjective such as *bad*. In some instances that would be true, e.g. *He felt the broken arm very carefully.* In our particular example, however, *feel* is operating as a copular or linking verb like *be*, *look*, *seem*, *taste*, etc., and should take an adjective just like other copular verbs, e.g.:

> He looks bad.
> It seems bad.
> It tastes bad.
> She is bad.

12.2   Because of the alternation between northern *past* **passt** [pæst] and southern **pahst** [pɑːst], some northern speakers may produce pseudo-southern **gahss-mahsk** [gɑːsmɑːsk] or even **gahss-massk** [gɑːsmæsk] rather than the genuine southern form **gass-mahsk** [gæsmɑːsk].

12.3   In American English, where a *t* occurs between two vowels, as in *city*, *better*, it is usually pronounced as a *d*: **ciddy**, **bedder**. In attempting to change American **d** to British **t** in words like this, some Americans may also overdo things and change the pronunciation of words like *ready* to **retty**.

12.4   The 'Bristol l' may have arisen as a result of speakers dropping the **l** at the end of words like *bottle* and *apple*, giving **botta** [bɒtə] and **appa** [æpə], and then, later, as a result of influence from 'posh' accents, reintroducing the **l** not only in words like *bottle* [bɒtəl] but also – over-doing things – in words like *America* [əmɛrɪkəl].

INDEX

The method of alphabetisation is word-by-word. An asterisk * marks definitions and explanations. *Italic* is used for page references to questions and/or answers. **Bold** is used for letters and words analysed for their sounds.